Fishing ONTARIO'S GRAND RIVER COUNTRY

EDITED BY STEPHEN MAY

FOR THE GRAND RIVER CONSERVATION AUTHORITY

LORIMER

JAMES LORIMER & COMPANY LTD., PUBLISHERS
TORONTO

James Lorimer & Company Ltd. acknowledges the support of
the Ontario Arts Council. We acknowledge the support of the
Government of Canada through the Canada Book Fund for our
publishing activities. We acknowledge the support of the Canada
Council for the Arts for our publishing program. We acknowledge
the assistance of the OMDC Book Fund, an initiative of the Ontario
Media Development Corporation.

Canada Council   Conseil des Arts
for the Arts   du Canada

ONTARIO ARTS COUNCIL
CONSEIL DES ARTS DE L'ONTARIO

Cover design by Meghan Collins

Library and Archives Canada Cataloguing in Publication

Fishing Ontario's Grand River country / edited by Stephen May
for the Grand River Conservation Authority.

ISBN 978-1-55277-468-7

1. Fishing—Ontario—Grand River—Guidebooks. 2. Grand
River
(Ont.)—Guidebooks. I. May, Stephen, 1967- II. Grand River
Conservation Authority

SH572.O5F495 2010   799.1'1097134   C2009-907093-6

James Lorimer & Company Ltd., Publishers
317 Adelaide Street West, Suite 1002
Toronto, Ontario
M5V 1P9
www.lorimer.ca

Printed in China

PHOTO CREDITS

Aaron Todd: 139; Bob Scott:
79, 82; Carl Hiebert: 22, 61,
128, 130; Dean McFadden: 113,
115; Grand River Conservation
Authority Collection: 12, 13, 36,
45, 69, 70, 73, 85, 86, 90, 99,
103, 107, 121, 141, 143; Jason
Forde: 65; Ken Collins: 78; Ken
Ingrham-Smith: 110, 118, 122;
Larry Halyk: cover, 9; Stephen
May: 14, 15, 16, 17, 18, 25, 27,
28, 30, 32, 33, 39, 43, 44, 47,
49, 52, 55, 59, 63, 65, 66, 77,
81, 94, 95, 107, 117, 124, 132,
136, 146, 147, 150, 151, 152,
154, 156; Todd Currie: 40; Dave
Schultz: 102; Derek Strub:
32; Mike Pettigrew: 91; Rob
Culp: 104; Warren Yerex: 96

Fishing Ontario's Grand River Country
is dedicated to the children who will grow
up to enjoy the Grand River valley.

Table of Contents

List of Maps

Foreword

If you are looking for a great place to wet a line, look no further than southern Ontario's Grand River. I've spent a lot of time fishing in this area and it has always been time well spent. The diversity of fish found in Grand River country means that there is usually something biting.

The mix of river, reservoirs, and tributaries means there is something for everyone. If you like to work offshore humps for walleye and smallmouth bass, cast dry flies for picky trout or hook up with feisty channel cats, Grand River Country has what you are looking for. It is no wonder that people travel from near and far to fish this area. In fact, I have featured the quality angling in the Grand River area on several episodes of my *Real Fishing Show*.

The people who care for this river are a big part of why this close to home fishery is so good. The partners of the Grand River Fisheries Management Plan Implementation Committee include volunteers, landowners, agency staff, and business owners who work together to improve the river and its fishery. Their award-winning efforts will be appreciated by anglers for years to come. Even this book is being used to help the fishing. Proceeds from *Fishing Ontario's Grand River Country* will help pay for river improvement projects through the Grand River Conservation Foundation.

I hope you will enjoy this book and your Grand fishing experiences.

Good luck and Real Fishing,

Bob Izumi

Acknowledgements

This edition of *Fishing Ontario's Grand River Country* is the result of a passion and a commitment to this wonderful river on the part of a number of special people. I would like to thank Derek Strub and Warren Yerex, whose editing and keen interest in the fishery over the past several years have been captured in these pages. Their willingness to share their experience with this fishery is truly appreciated.

This book would not have been possible without the assistance and advice of many other supporters of the Grand River fishery. Rob Baldwin, Felix Barbetti, Ken Collins, Ray Collesso, Rob Culp, Paul General, Larry Halyk, Jack Imhof, Tom MacDougall, Dean McFadden, Larry McGratton, Larry Mellors, Al Murray, Mike Pettigrew, Art Timmerman, Mitch Wilson, and many others all helped to build an understanding of what this fishery has to offer from source to mouth. Their commitment to the fishery and the environment in the Grand River valley — one of the best places to live in Ontario — is deeply appreciated.

This book was built on the foundation of *Fishing Grand River Country*, published in 1990. This first edition was written by Liz Leedham and Jim Reid, with help from Rob Baldwin, Derek Strub, Warren Yerex, and a wide variety of people dedicated to the Grand River fishery, its protection, enhancement, and promotion. Additional support for this edition came from folks at the GRCA, including Ralph Beaumont, Dave Schultz, Lara Vujanic, and Carol Bystriansky.

Last but not least, my family has helped me develop a deeper appreciation for this river. Trips along the river with Sarah, Ryan, and Kathy have helped me better understand why I am passionate about the Grand River environment that we call home.

Steve May

WELCOME TO GRAND RIVER COUNTRY

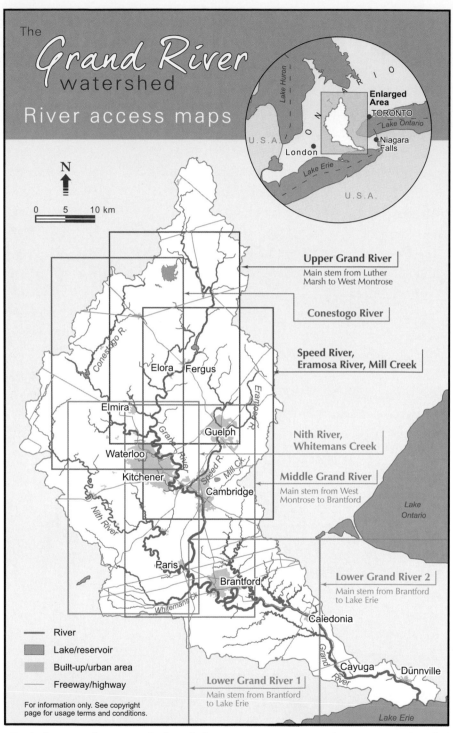

The Grand River watershed

River access maps

Enlarged Area
TORONTO
London
Niagara Falls
U.S.A.
Lake Huron
Lake Ontario
Lake Erie
U.S.A.

N

0   5   10 km

Upper Grand River
Main stem from Luther Marsh to West Montrose

Conestogo River

Speed River,
Eramosa River, Mill Creek

Nith River,
Whitemans Creek

Middle Grand River
Main stem from West Montrose to Brantford

Lower Grand River 2
Main stem from Brantford to Lake Erie

Lower Grand River 1
Main stem from Brantford to Lake Erie

Conestogo R.
Elora   Fergus
Eramosa R.
Elmira
Grand River
Guelph
Waterloo
Speed R.   Mill Ck.
Kitchener
Cambridge
Nith River
Lake Ontario
Paris
Brantford
Whitemans Ck.
Caledonia
Cayuga   Dunnville
Grand River
Lake Erie

River
Lake/reservoir
Built-up/urban area
Freeway/highway

For information only. See copyright page for usage terms and conditions.

Each box on this watershed-scale locator map corresponds to a more detailed access-point map reproduced later in this book.

WELCOME TO GRAND RIVER COUNTRY

Anglers living in the urban areas of this country are usually looking for great fishing spots close to home. Places that are scenic and have a healthy population of willing fish are especially sought after. People in southern Ontario need not look much further than the Grand River.

The Grand flows through the heart of southern Ontario, and getting to the river requires a less than one-hour drive for over six million people. Expand that to a two-hour radius, and over fourteen million people have easy access to the Grand's diverse and productive waters. So how is the fishing in this urban area? Better than ever!

The Grand River is located just west of the Golden Horseshoe. It starts close to Georgian Bay in the high land around Dundalk, and flows 300 km (186 mi) south, through picturesque farms, wetlands, forests, and cities before entering Lake Erie at Port Maitland. The Grand flows right through the cities of Kitchener–Waterloo, Cambridge, Guelph, and Brantford. On its journey, it is joined by four major tributaries: the Nith, Conestogo, Speed, and Eramosa rivers. The many faces of the Grand River include swift cold-water trout streams; serene pastoral stretches, filled with smallmouth, pike, and walleye; and big-river fishing for anything from rainbow trout to crappies. In fact, over half of the fish species in Canada call the Grand River home.

Residents of the Grand River watershed have good reason to be proud of the Grand River and its tributaries. Because of its significant human heritage and excellent recreation opportunities, the Grand River system was proclaimed a Canadian Heritage River in 1994. It is the first urbanized river in Canada to achieve this status.

Grand River Country in southern Ontario has something for all of us: great scenery; history; theatre; music; farmers' markets; fine dining; canoeing, hiking, and cycling trails; and some of the best recreational fishing in eastern North America.

To find out more about watershed tourism and attractions, contact: Grand River Country at 866-900-4722 or visit us online at www.grandrivercountry.com.

Droughts were common in the 1930s as can be seen here in downtown Paris.

A Not So "Grand" Past

Things were not always as good as they are today in the Grand River watershed. In the Grand River area we are truly living the "Good Old Days" right now. Through the 1800s and most of the 1900s, you couldn't fish for healthy populations of brown trout, rainbow trout, walleye, smallmouth bass, channel catfish, or northern pike in most of the watershed. But now you can!

The Grand River's history reveals how abuse of the environment can have devastating effects on fish populations. During pre-European settlement, the watershed was over 95 per cent forested. According to archaeological studies, there were extensive wetlands in the headwaters area of the Grand. During this time, species like brook trout, lake sturgeon, walleye, perch, bass, muskellunge, and blue pickerel (now extinct) were all abundant in the river.

After two hundred years of settlement in this area, the river changed. Forest clearing, swamp draining, dams, dumping of all types of waste into the river, and settlement in the floodplain combined to create a much different river. From the late 1800s through the 1940s, the Grand was a river you could usually smell before you could see. Its alternating flooding and drought conditions were a concern for local residents, because of the property damage the river could inflict and the public-safety issue associated

May 1974 flood in Kitchener.

with low flows during summer dry periods. At these times parts of the river often included more raw sewage than water.

Things were so bad that a 1966 survey identified that there were no longer any smallmouth bass or northern pike upstream of Brantford. People did not let their children go near the water for fear of illness, and articles in the *Kitchener–Waterloo Record* bluntly called the river an open sewer. It really wasn't a pretty place, let alone somewhere to enjoy fishing.

ROAD TO RECOVERY

Given such a level of degradation, a commitment was made to improve the river, and people began thinking about how to make the river's future brighter. Significant work to address public-health and safety concerns actually began in the 1930s. Many of these improvements to water quality and river levels have provided a huge benefit to the river's fish populations.

Some of the first improvements involved the building of water-control dams for flood control, water supply, and water quality. The Grand River Conservation Authority (GRCA) and its precursors have worked with government agencies and municipalities to solve these long-standing problems.

Ontario Stewardship Rangers complete a river cleanup in downtown Fergus.

The Shand Dam, built in 1942 near Fergus, was the first structure installed to reduce flood damage and to provide more consistent flows through summer low-flow periods. Other dams followed in the watershed, which helped the Grand River Conservation Authority better manage the problem. These dams now provide numerous benefits to the watershed. They reduce flood flows, ensure minimum flows through dry summers, and provide high-quality fisheries in the reservoirs and tailwater areas below these dams. The moderated flows have helped many fish populations blossom.

Other GRCA programs have contributed to a reduction of once-severe flooding and an enormous improvement in water quality. In addition to the dams, the GRCA has regulated floodplain development, planted over twenty-five million trees, helped the agricultural community with best-management farming practices to reduce pollution, and built erosion-control works in many municipalities. Numerous landowners, fishing clubs, and other volunteers have also contributed time and effort to stream and fishery improvements.

Additional "on-the-ground" programs, offered by government, by not-for-profit organizations, and by landowners, have also had a significant impact on water quality and habitat. Large-scale tree-planting programs, improvements to agricultural practices, and sewage-treatment-plant upgrades have all contributed to steady improvement in fish habitat and water quality. The Grand River Watershed Plan and various municipal

A large-scale structural enhancement project is underway on the Grand River tailwater.

master plans are all working towards this common goal of improving water quality, which helps wildlife habitat and fish populations.

GRAND RIVER FISHERIES MANAGEMENT PLAN

A unique cooperative arrangement that is making a difference is the Grand River Fisheries Management Plan (GRFMP). The planning process initiated in 1995 was "community-based" and involved fisheries managers from various agencies and representatives from the public and many NGOs. These people all worked together to complete the GRFMP by 1998.

This cooperative living document was created by all of the stakeholders in the fishery, including many active volunteers and business owners, who were at the table on an equal footing with government agency staff while the plan was being initiated, built, and implemented. The plan literally started with a blank piece of paper in a room where all of the key stakeholders were present. The Fisheries Management Plan provides direction on how the fishery and the land base can be managed to benefit future generations.

The plan identifies forty-two recommendations or "Best Bets," designed to improve the fishery in this river system. An Implementation Committee

Education is a big part of fisheries management.

is now in place, working towards completing these "Best Bets." Since 1998, the plan partners have contributed over six million dollars to address the plan's recommendations.

The strength of the Grand River Fisheries Management Plan is that it presents a balanced approach, relying on dedicated volunteers, with their community ties and grassroots knowledge, along with technical expertise from agency staff. The GRFMP provides guidance on managing the fish resources and overall environmental health of the Grand River watershed. The GRFMP is both a stand-alone document and an integral part of the overall Watershed Plan.

Of course, there is still a long way to go to realize all the recommendations outlined, but the Fisheries Management Plan and Watershed Plan for this river are well on their way to being implemented, and the results are becoming more evident every year.

A GRAND FUTURE

The efforts by a wide variety of partners to improve the river and its fishery are an inspiration to volunteers and agency staff. The "canaries in the coal mine" for the Grand River are the fish. What has been found in recent assessments is that the Grand River now has a very diverse and healthy fish community. Over two-thirds of the fish species in Ontario are found in the Grand watershed, and some of the rarest species in the country call the

Walleye research in the lower reaches of the river has helped managers better address the needs of this popular game fish.

Grand River home. But, there are still areas of concern. Excessive nutrients from upstream are limiting the environmental improvements in the lower reaches of the river, and development pressures continue to stress many areas in the Grand River watershed. Continued efforts by the various "friends of the fishery" are needed to see continued improvement to the environment and fishery in this region.

The Grand now boasts a world-class brown-trout fishery that attracts fly fishers from around the world, quality steelhead fishing that rivals any river in the Great Lakes region and many West Coast waters, abundant river smallmouth, and excellent fishing for walleye, channel catfish, carp, and a host of other species, all of which are found throughout the watershed in a scenic and natural environment.

GRAND RIVER CONSERVATION FOUNDATION

If you fish, you know that the Grand River and its tributaries provide some of Ontario's best fishing! Many of the notable improvements in fish habitat and water quality have been funded by the Grand River Conservation Foundation (GRCF).

Ken Collins and some happy anglers from the Ministry of Tourism on the Grand River.

For more than forty years, the GRCF has worked hand-in-hand with the GRCA to produce a better quality of life for the residents of the Grand River watershed. The foundation's goal is to respond to watershed needs, by marshalling concerned volunteers who have a passion for nature and the outdoors.

The foundation's Grand Champions Clean Water Action Fund supports the efforts of the Grand River Fisheries Management Plan Implementation Committee and their projects to improve fishing and river water quality. Your purchase of this book supports stream rehabilitation projects, tree planting, water-quality research, river-access improvements, and the reduction of river pollution.

The GRCF also makes grants to schools, community groups, and others that help finance projects that benefit our environment and the fishery of the Grand River. Funds for these grants come from the Thiess Riverprize Fund — won by the GRCA in 2000, when it was named the world's top watershed-management agency — and the Grand Champions Endowment Fund.

The foundation is now integrating and supporting day-to-day programs that benefit the people and wildlife of our watershed, as well as the Grand River and its fishery. The foundation also aims to expand its network of volunteers from communities throughout the watershed, with the goal of creating "local ambassadors" who have a passion for nature, conservation, and active living in their community.

If you enjoy fishing, hiking, walking, cycling, or canoeing along the Grand River, you can support these and other important community river projects even further — with a tax-deductible donation. If you have questions about becoming a volunteer, please contact:

Grand River Conservation Foundation
519-621-2761 ext 2272
400 Clyde Rd., PO Box 729, Cambridge, Ontario N1R 5W6
Charitable Registration Number 11894 6045 RR0001

Thank you for making a difference!
www.grcf.ca
foundation@grandriver.ca

ABOUT THIS BOOK

This book is designed to help you explore the fisheries resources found in the Grand River watershed. To do this the book has been divided into sections that describe this large, diverse watershed. Each section uses maps, charts, and descriptions to help you take advantage of the fishing resources found in the area. Each has a "finder map" and one or more maps of the individual locations being described. These maps will help you find the major access points by road or river and indicate some of the fishy features of the present. Each section identifies what species anglers can expect to find and the best times to target each species. Safety considerations, public access points, and fishing tips are found in the text descriptions of each area.

The main stem of the Grand really changes as it flows from the Dundalk Highlands down through to Lake Erie, from Belwood Lake and its tail-water's world-renowned trout fishery, which is best accessed by wading, to the canoe-friendly Exceptional Waters Area and the big-water diversity of the Southern Grand River. The main stem of the Grand and all the major access points and information on how to hook up with many species of fish are described in the first section.

The second section deals with the Grand's tributaries. The Conestogo River, Nith River, Whitemans Creek, and the Speed/Eramosa System are all excellent fisheries that feed into the Grand. The unique attributes of these systems are also described, with maps, tables, and descriptions based on the experiences of long-time local anglers to help you explore these wonderful places.

On the Grand River, canoeing and fishing go hand-in-hand. For serious canoeists, we recommend *Paddling the Grand River*, which has a more thorough description of the paddling and canoe-access opportunities on the main stem of the Grand.

FISHING REGULATIONS IN THE GRAND RIVER WATERSHED

In the province of Ontario, all residents between the ages of eighteen and sixty-five require a valid fishing licence to fish. All non-residents must also have a valid fishing licence to angle in the province of Ontario.

Seasons and limits apply to the entire Grand River watershed, and they vary by species. Fisheries Management Zone (FMZ) #16 covers the entire Grand River watershed, and its general regulations apply for most of the watershed. However, there are some notable fisheries in the Grand River basin that have special regulations in place to protect significant fisheries. These regulations apply mainly for trout fishing in the Fergus–Elora area, for Whitemans Creek near Brantford, and for the walleye fishery downstream of Brantford. On the Grand River, in parts of the Exceptional Waters area between Paris and Brantford, catch-and-release regulations are in place for all species and, in the lower portions of the river, walleye seasons and limits may be different from the rest of FMZ #16. For details and up-to date information about fishing regulations in the Grand River, please refer to the Ministry of Natural Resources' website or consult the *Ontario Recreational Fishing Regulations Summary*, available without cost at most outfitters and tackle shops in Ontario.

RIVER FLOW RATES

Rivers are dynamic, and flow rates change. Releases from the major reservoirs, excessive rainfall, and snow melt can all quickly increase water levels in the Grand River system. Anglers need to be aware of the fact that, as water levels rise, the river can get increasingly dangerous. To find out the current river levels, the "River Data" section of the GRCA's website at www.grandriver.ca is very useful. If the flows have recently increased, you should take additional caution when fishing on the river or on shore, when wading, or when in a boat. The descriptions of the fishing locations may also identify known hazards in the river, such as dams and weirs. Anglers wading or in boats should be aware of these and treat them with extreme caution. Each year people lose their lives in the waters of the Grand River watershed. Be careful and respectful of the dangers posed by flowing waters and you should have a safe and enjoyable experience on the Grand.

Some things you can do to help keep yourself safe include:
- Being aware of dams and weirs, and portaging around them, using the designated sites;
- Always wearing your PFD when in a boat or canoe on the river or in reservoirs;
- Taking extra caution when the waters are cold;

The marshes near the mouth of the Grand are important for Lake Erie and river fish.

- Wading carefully and never wading alone;
- Using a wading staff and avoiding wading where you cannot see bottom;
- Watching children carefully around water;
- Checking the GRCA website (www.grandriver.ca) to see what the flow levels are before your next adventure on the Grand.

RIVER ACCESS

Most of the sites listed in this publication are formal public access sites. Nevertheless some access points are privately owned. Some of them, such as conservation areas, also have associated service fees for access. The main and most popular access points to various fishing locations are listed in each section of the book, but access points can be closed without notice for many different reasons. Note that there are additional access points constantly being developed by partners of the Grand River Fisheries Management Plan and by various municipalities. For updates to access points, refer to the GRCA's website at www.grandriver.ca.

Species	Jan	Feb	Mar	Apr	May	June	July	Aug	Sept	Oct	Nov	Dec
Bass						*	*	*	*	•		
Pike	•	•	*		*	•	•	•	•	•		
Carp				•	*	*	*	•	•			

The charts in each section of this book are designed to let you know when various species are in season and when fishing for that species is usually the best. An asterisk means the species is available during the month shown, but fishing may be mediocre. A bullet means it is a prime time to target that species. The seasons for each fish do not always fully align with the month, and data could not always be provided for every species in every area. Please check to ensure the season for the species you are seeking is open by checking the Ministry of Natural Resources' *2010 Ontario Recreational Fishing Regulations Summary*.

Fish Species of the Grand River

The Grand River is home to a wide assortment of fish. Some eighty-two species currently call this river home, including a variety of minnows and non-game fish species. This is about half of all the species found in Canada, and many are very popular sport fish. The Grand, despite its near-urban location is a well-known fishery that provides quality angling opportunities for people targeting walleye, rainbow trout, smallmouth bass, brown trout, and many more. Below is a brief summary of some of the more popular fish in the river and some tips to get you hooked up.

Smallmouth Bass

 Bass are right at home through much of the Grand, because many areas in the watershed consist of steadily flowing waters with frequent riffles and pools, flowing over largely limestone-based river bottoms. This type of river provides perfect habitat for smallmouth.

The Grand River is a bass factory. From the cities of Kitchener and Waterloo, downstream through Cambridge, Brantford, and Caledonia, the river's fertile waters provide perfect habitat for river bass, which feed heavily on minnows, crayfish, and aquatic insects. The fish in this area are often smaller than their lake or reservoir counterparts, but their abundance can make up for their size. Using light tackle or fly gear is an ideal way to enjoy this easy-to-reach fishery.

Many areas of the Grand, Conestogo, and Nith rivers are also good river-bass fisheries that are often under-used. Healthy populations provide great sport in rivers if you scale down your tackle appropriately. They are perfect for fly-rod enthusiasts and anglers using ultra-light spinning gear and downsized lures. River bass, by their very nature, are usually more aggressive than their lake counterparts. Fish in lakes and reservoirs reach larger sizes faster, due to a longer growing season.

In addition to the productive river fisheries, the reservoirs provide exceptional bass fishing. The Conestogo, Guelph, and Belwood reservoirs contain very good populations of smallmouth. Being reservoirs that are

Smallmouth bass are found throughout the Grand and its tributaries.

used for flow augmentation and flood control, they can fish differently than a usual lake. Since there are variable water levels and a lack of shoreline aquatic vegetation, these fish often relate to offshore humps, river channels, and old roadbeds. Anglers used to fishing using sonar to find the hidden hotspots on a lake bottom can do exceptionally well with these reservoir bass populations.

In this part of Ontario, smallmouth bass season is closed from the end of November through to the fourth Saturday in June. Please refer to the Ministry of Natural Resources' *2010 Ontario Recreational Fishing Regulations Summary* to ensure you are fishing legally. It is illegal to target smallmouth bass when the fishing season is closed. This also applies to catch-and-release fishing.

LARGEMOUTH BASS

Largemouth are found in all of the reservoirs, but they are most prominent in Shade's Mills Reservoir, Conestogo Lake, Rockwood Reservoir, and Guelph Lake. There are also isolated pockets of largemouth bass in the main stem of the river and in many of the floodplain ponds, such as those found in the Kitchener–Waterloo area. Largemouth are usually an incidental catch for anglers who are targeting other species, but people who fish typical largemouth habitats in the reservoirs and lower portions of the river will find them.

WALLEYE

This species is highly sought after throughout Canada. In the Grand River watershed there are a few distinct walleye fisheries that anglers will want to target if they enjoy battling and eating quality walleye.

The lower portions of the river, from Brantford downstream to Lake Erie, are home to migratory walleye that use the eastern basin of Lake Erie for foraging and the river as a spawning and nursery habitat. The lower reaches of the Grand River have an immediate connection to Lake Erie. This provides a rare opportunity to fish for large walleye from shore or from a small boat. These migratory fish also provide some great angling opportunities, since such larger walleye would normally be targeted with big-water boats and downriggers.

Resident river populations of walleye are found in various portions of the watershed. The Nith River has resident fish downstream of New Hamburg. The Conestogo River near St. Jacobs produces walleye regularly, and the main stem of the Grand River downstream of Paris also has a small resident walleye population.

Two reservoirs in the watershed hold walleye. The Conestogo Lake Reservoir has walleye, due to a Ministry of Natural Resources (MNR) initiative to transfer fish from the lower reaches of the watershed into this suitable habitat. Walleye have also been found in Belwood Reservoir. These fish are of unknown origin, but a quality fishery is emerging in the reservoir and in the river below the Shand Dam.

NORTHERN PIKE

Northern-pike fishing in the Grand River watershed can be surprisingly good, considering the near-urban location. Pike are often associated with remote areas in the far north, but the Grand and its reservoirs hold solid populations of these aggressive fish. The Grand has both river and reservoir populations of northerns that are worth targeting.

This walleye uses both the river and Lake Erie as habitat.

In the reservoirs you can find pike at Belwood, Conestogo, Guelph, and Shade's Mills. Belwood and Conestogo lakes are known for their trophy pike fishing, and fish over one metre (forty inches long) are caught at these lakes each season. The other reservoirs have good populations of fish as well. Pike are easiest to find in the spring, shortly after the season opens in mid-May. Northerns are ambush predators, and flooded willows found at most of the reservoirs at this time of year provide perfect pike habitat. As the reservoir levels decrease through the summer, pike switch to offshore humps and gravel bars to forage. These locations are not as obvious as the flooded willows, and during the summer these fish tend to roam quite a bit. In the fall, pike often move to shallower areas to feed, in preparation for winter. Ice fishing for pike is popular on some of the reservoirs, and ice-hut rentals are available at Belwood Lake.

In the river there are good populations of pike, but these populations can vary from year to year, and river fishing for pike is less consistent. Areas to target are deeper pools and bay mouths that lead to areas flooded in the spring. Early in the season, pike will not be far from flooded areas, because this is the type of habitat that river pike require for spawning. During the summer, the bottom of deeper holes and backwaters behind dams are good locations for pike, as are areas where minnows are concentrated. Prime pike water on the Grand can be found in the Grand River Tailwater and through Kitchener–Waterloo. They are also found throughout the rest of the main stem of the Grand River all the way to Lake Erie, but they are

Steelhead are a popular fish targeted with a variety of tackle.

not as common once you get downstream of Cambridge. Other places to look for pike are in the Conestogo River above and below the Conestogo Reservoir and in the Speed River, below the City of Guelph to the confluence with the Grand River.

RAINBOW TROUT (STEELHEAD)

 Migratory rainbow trout, or steelhead, have flourished in the Grand River since the removal of the Lorne Dam in Brantford in 1989. The removal of this obstacle allowed rainbows to access quality spawning waters found in tributaries upstream of Brantford. Whitemans Creek and several tributaries of the Nith River are all producing good numbers of rainbow smolts, which travel out to Lake Erie to feed and grow. When these wild fish return to the Grand, they are large and healthy. Anglers fishing through the fall in the main stem of the Grand River below the town of Paris all the way through to past the village of York find these fish regularly.

Strong-run wild steelhead easily negotiate the Dunnville Dam and the dam in Caledonia. Fishing below these two obstacles and Wilkes Dam in Brantford is productive. The fish that make it to the Brantford area and the Exceptional Waters reach are exceptional fish that have run over 128 km (80 river mi) from Lake Erie. The beautiful waters in the Exceptional Waters reach lend themselves to fly fishing in the traditional West Coast style. Wide-open pools and beautiful scenery have more anglers trying their luck in this area every season.

This evolving steelhead fishery has attracted fly anglers who enjoy using two-handed, or "Spey"-type, tackle. There have been two "Spey Claves," where fly fishers from around North America have gathered to learn about this type of fishing and to try for the river's steelhead. This portion of the Grand River provides ideal conditions for this style of fishing. The long, soft water pools hold fish and make swinging a fly with a two-handed rod an efficient way to search out steelhead. In fact, this is one of the very best areas this side of the Rockies to Spey fish for wild steelhead.

An extended season for rainbow trout has been implemented in the Grand River downstream of Paris to Lake Erie. This allows anglers to target these fish during their fall migrations. The season is closed from January 1 through to the fourth Saturday in April to protect spawning fish. In late April, some steelhead still remain in the river and, in years when the water conditions are right, good steelhead fishing can be had into May.

BROWN TROUT

The most publicized fishery in the Grand is the tailwater brown-trout fishery found below the Shand Dam at Lake Belwood. The Grand River Tailwater, flowing through the towns of Fergus and Elora, has put the Grand River on the world's trout-fishing map. Below the Shand Dam, about 20 km (12 mi) of excellent trout water can be found. In the tailwater area, phenomenal insect hatches and a beautiful river corridor combine to make this a prime brown-trout angling destination. Here the brown trout are protected by special regulations, attracting anglers from around the world.

The Conestogo Tailwater is a fledgling fishery, where the conditions are similar to the tailwater near Fergus and Elora. This is a river to watch in the future. The Conestogo Tailwater is also a productive trout fishery for about

A Grand River brown.

15 km (9 mi) downstream from the Conestogo Dam. The landscape in the Conestogo River valley is more open and rural, but the fishing can be good. In 2006, the Canadian Fly Fishing Championships were held on the Grand and Conestogo rivers, attesting to the quality of these fisheries. Catch rates were slightly higher on the Conestogo River.

In addition to the tailwater fisheries, which are supported by annual stocking by the Ministry of Natural Resources and a group of volunteers, are smaller rivers that have naturally reproducing brown trout. Mill Creek from Guelph to Cambridge holds wild brown trout, as does Whitemans Creek near Burford. The upper Eramosa River has a solid population, and Laurel Creek near Waterloo has some brown trout, but access to many of these waters requires landowner permission.

BROOK TROUT

This species is the "canary in the coal mine" for the Grand River watershed. This native trout requires high-quality cold-water environments to survive, and there are good populations in many areas of the watershed. However, almost all of these ideal habitats are smaller creeks and streams flowing through private lands. Because of this limited access, the brook trout is not an important game-fish species. Nevertheless, if you go to the upper reaches of the Speed, Eramosa, and Nith rivers, and other tributaries of the Grand River — especially in Waterloo Region, Wellington County, and Dufferin County — you can find good brookie water on private property that can be accessed — if you get the landowner's permission.

CRAPPIE

This panfish species is sought after because of its eating qualities and the fact that the fish often school together, making good catches possible. Crappies are found in Guelph Lake and Shade's Mills Reservoir. The crappie in the Corrections Ponds in Guelph are also a popular target for anglers. In addition, crappie are found at various locations in the main river, from Waterloo downstream. Areas to look for are back bays with some depth and creek mouths, particularly if woody debris and deeper holes are present. Small minnows and jigs suspended under a small float are top baits throughout the Grand from Kitchener–Waterloo down to Lake Erie. The regions above and below Caledonia are especially productive waters for white crappie.

CHANNEL CATFISH

Channel cats are a great game fish that are readily available for anglers fishing the Grand River downstream of Brantford. Cats are best targeted with bait such as dead minnows, worms, and stink baits designed for catfish. Fishing on the bottom near dark is a very effective strategy. Look for these whiskered battlers upstream and downstream of both the Caledonia and Dunnville dams. Catfish prefer some current and deeper pockets of water or large pools.

Perch are tasty when pulled through the ice at Belwood Lake.

CARP

In much of Canada this species does not get a lot of respect. However, carp are an intelligent fish that can take considerable skill to catch. They are also very strong and fight hard when hooked. This is a prime sport fish in Europe, and it is gaining in popularity in North America. The Grand River is home to good populations of this species, and anglers looking for something different can target carp with a variety of baits. Worms can be effective, but canned corn and dough balls are often more productive. Many anglers make their own baits, or "boilies" as they are often called, and have elaborate chum recipes to attract these fish to an angler's bait. Experienced carp anglers from Europe will have a field day with the Grand River's uneducated fish. For a real challenge, try targeting carp that are cruising in shallow water, using fly tackle and a small crayfish or nymph pattern. The Grand River offers almost endless opportunities for anglers looking for good carp fishing.

MAIN STEM OF THE GRAND RIVER

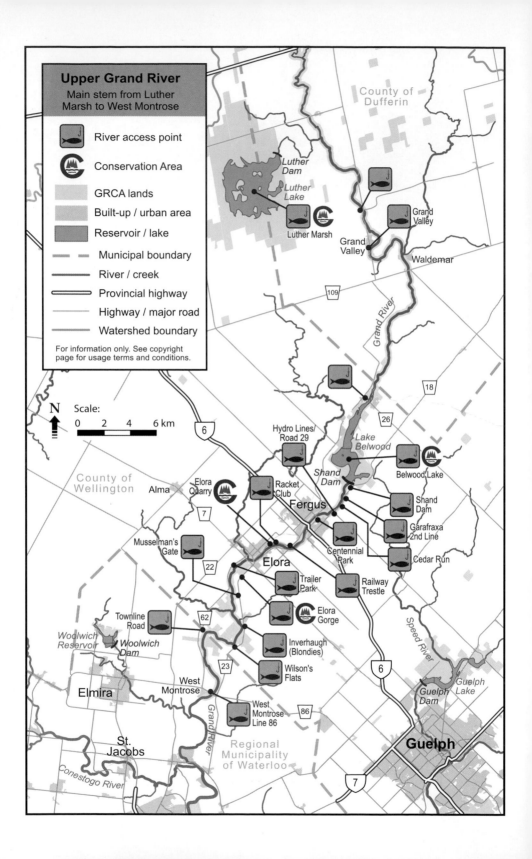

UPPER GRAND RIVER: LUTHER LAKE TO BELWOOD

SPECIES: Smallmouth bass, northern pike, carp, panfish

Species	Jan	Feb	Mar	Apr	May	June	July	Aug	Sept	Oct	Nov	Dec
Pike					*	*	•	•	•	•	•	
Bass						•	•	•	•	•	•	
Carp				•	•	•	•	•	•			

FISHING HIGHLIGHTS: In this area the Grand is a small river, best accessed by wading. Keep things light and enjoy the peaceful surroundings and the small, but usually eager, fish.

PUBLIC ACCESS: Grand Valley, bridge crossings

FISHING THE UPPER GRAND RIVER

Upstream of Belwood Lake the Grand River, still a small stream, is home to smallmouth bass, northern pike, carp, and a variety of minnow species. The river is characterized by riffles and pools flowing over bedrock and broken gravel.

The deep holes that are relatively common on this reach of river are good spots to find fish of surprising quality, considering the size of the stream of origin. Don't expect monster fish, but they are often eager, because they are lightly fished. Using light tackle or a fly rod is the way to go to get the most sport out of the fish found here. Small panfish poppers can be a lot of fun. Small surface flies are often eagerly attacked by the bass of the area. To find larger fish, try a small plug or streamer fly fished in deeper water. Areas where the current flows into deeper pools can be real hot spots. To catch numbers of fish, it is tough to beat a small nymph on a fly rod or a piece of worm under a float with a spinning rod. The best way to get at these fish is by wading the river. If the water is warm, as it usually is during bass season,

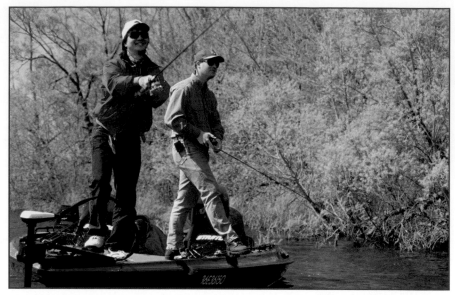

Anglers enjoy the larger reservoirs for bass, pike and walleye action.

this is a pleasant way to spend a few hours fishing. Wear a pair of sneakers that you don't mind getting wet and a pair of shorts.

Fishing near bridges that cross the Grand is a good bet, as there are often deeper holes near the bridge abutments. You can also knock on the doors of farmers whose property is dissected by the river. This small stream is largely on private property, so gaining access can take a bit of work. But it can be fun to explore an area that is lightly fished.

The area around Grand Valley is popular with some local anglers, and the bridges just upstream of Belwood Lake also offer fishing opportunities. There are no formal access points in this portion of the Grand River. Nevertheless, there is a roadside park in Grand Valley that does have some good-looking water running through it.

SIGHTS TO SEE: There is a large wind farm in this area that is generating green power and, in spring or fall, you can see large numbers of migrating birds passing through the Luther Marsh area.

Belwood Lake Conservation Area

SPECIES: Smallmouth bass, northern pike, yellow perch, walleye, bullhead, carp

Species	Jan	Feb	Mar	Apr	May	June	July	Aug	Sept	Oct	Nov	Dec
Bass						*	*	*	*	*	*	
Perch	*	*	•	*	*	*	*	•	•	*	*	*
Pike	*	*			*	*	*	•	•	*	*	
Walleye	*	*	*		*	*	*	*	*	*	*	*
Carp				*	*	*	•	•	•	•		

FISHING HIGHLIGHTS: Belwood Lake offers good fishing for pike, bass, walleye, and perch. Some of the best fishing is accessed by boat, and a good launch facility is available at the conservation area, where shore fishing can also be good at certain times of the year. Spring and summer are prime times for pike, while fishing for smallmouth bass and walleye is strong in the summer and fall. Carp anglers do well throughout the spring season. When ice conditions are safe, winter anglers can access good pike and perch fishing. The conservation area provides minnows as well as ice-hut and boat rentals. Belwood Lake contour maps are available at the park gatehouse.

PUBLIC ACCESS: Belwood Lake Conservation Area provides a boat-launch area (fees apply).

FISHING BELWOOD LAKE CONSERVATION AREA

Belwood Lake is a deep, 12-km (7.5-mi) long reservoir created by the Shand Dam on the Grand River northeast of Fergus. It is a half-hour drive from Kitchener–Waterloo, Cambridge, and Guelph, and about one and a half hours from Toronto and London. Take Wellington Road #18 east of Fergus to the Belwood Lake Conservation Area entrance. This scenic reservoir is home to good populations of northern pike, smallmouth bass, walleye, and perch. A brown-trout fishery exists below the Shand Dam (see Fergus section). Here the GRCA owns 1,348 hectares (3,330 acres), which include the 758-ha (1,874-ac) lake. Boat access to the lake is provided by two concrete launches. Powerboating is permitted, and park entry and boat-launch fees apply. The conservation area is open year round, but access to the lake may be restricted if conditions are unsafe.

Spring and early summer are prime times for some tremendous pike fishing in Belwood Lake. Pike spawn in late March through April, and by the time pike season opens in mid-May, they are aggressive and feeding actively. The reservoir water levels are fairly high at this time of year, flooding the shoreline and some willow-covered islands. Pike use these flooded trees as feeding and ambush areas, feeding heavily on baitfish and small fish such as perch.

The key to success on Belwood is to match your lure to the forage base. Casting brightly coloured spinnerbaits (white or chartreuse) in and along the flooded willows will trigger the pike to hit. Natural and bright jerkbaits and minnow baits in the 10-cm-to-17-cm (4-in-to-7-in) range, cast parallel to the willows and brought in on an erratic retrieve, will interest good numbers of pike.

After periods of poor weather or when a cold front moves through, pike often get sluggish and more finicky. When this occurs, switch over to slow-moving baits such as soft plastic jerkbaits, baited jigs, or a slow-running crankbait trolled in deeper water just off willow-covered shorelines.

Smallmouth bass fishing in Belwood Lake can be excellent. Concentrate on long, sloping gravel and rubble points, river channel bends, and mid-lake humps. These areas are perfect for topwater action in the morning and evening hours, using a variety of lures such as poppers and floating minnow baits. During the day, cast brightly coloured crankbaits and/or naturally coloured grubs and tubes. Salted tube jigs are a special favourite among

Derek Strub and a quality pike at Belwood Lake.

Belwood smallies, and should be fished slowly along the bottom.

Pike fishing can be good in the summer. Concentrate on areas near where the willows were submerged in the spring. The trees will now be high and dry, but the pike will not be far away. Look for pike holding on mid-lake structures, such as points, humps, and inside turns. The best tactics are to cast spinnerbaits, crankbaits, or larger jigs to these areas. Another good technique at this time of the year is to troll slowly in a zig-zag pattern along willow shorelines or creek channels. The best baits for trolling are large minnow baits.

Anglers hoping to target walleye in Belwood Lake should look for deeper humps and points and the old river channel. Working these areas with live-bait rigs, jigs, worm harnesses, and minnow baits can be quite productive. Walleye are also a common incidental catch of smallmouth anglers.

Fall is the time to find high-quality bass fishing, and provides an excellent chance for big fish. Most of the lake is deserted at this time of the year. Smallmouth bass begin to concentrate in the fall, and are very aggressive as they fatten for winter. Look for these strong-fighting fish around rocky points and humps. The key baits are brightly coloured crankbaits and jigs.

Belwood Lake has a solid smallmouth bass population.

Most anglers use an assortment of salted tube jigs and grubs in a variety of natural colours to get connected with Belwood bass.

Fall is also prime time for big pike. Try fishing along humps and points with big baits to attract big fish. Large jerkbaits in bright, gaudy colours are a favourite of experienced Belwood anglers. You may catch only a few pike each trip at this time, but they are usually high-quality fish. Many anglers also use live and dead minnows on quick-strike rigs to hook up with pike in the fall. Larger minnows are the way to go when targeting pike that are trying to put on some weight before winter. Large sucker minnows are especially popular.

When the reservoir freezes over, ice fishing is permitted when ice conditions are suitable. Many anglers concentrate on the lake's large perch population and occasionally hook into a pike. Live minnows and small jigs account for the majority of the perch caught through the ice. With perch fishing, it often pays to be mobile in order to track down roving schools of fish. Belwood can produce good numbers of jumbo perch if you get onto the right school, since fish of a similar size often travel together. Lucky and hard-working anglers can encounter fish in the 27-to-33-cm (11-to-13-in) range. The majority of Belwood perch are in the 15-to-22-cm (6-to-9-in) range. The most successful perch anglers on Belwood are mobile and drill a lot of holes. A small 11-to-15-cm (4.5-to-6-in) auger can be a real asset to a perch angler. Portable sonar can also help locate bottom structure that is attractive to perch. The former river channel and sloping points are often key features where fish concentrate.

Many anglers target pike with large minnows on tip-ups and large jigging lures. Fishing for pike is more often a game of waiting for the fish to come to you. The conservation area sells minnows and offers ice-hut rentals. The huts are placed in good pike habitat, close to the dam and first bay. Pike up to 76 cm (30 in) are commonly caught through the ice. In the winter, fishing is not allowed within 100 m (109 yd) of the dam wing walls.

WATER LEVELS: Belwood Lake is a large flood-control and water-supply facility operated by the Grand River Conservation Authority. Water levels are highest in the spring when the lake is filled with snowmelt and runoff. The levels drop gradually from the summer into the fall. In late fall, the lake is taken down to a winter level, which is quite low.

SIGHTS TO SEE: Belwood Lake Conservation Area is a day-use area that provides swimming, picnic areas, playground, boat launches, and wash-rooms. An admission fee is required, and no camping is permitted. Park facilities include boat rentals, the Hampton Barn Pavilion for large group rentals, a stocked trout pond for young anglers, and an annual Fly Fishing Forum.

MORE INFORMATION: Belwood Lake Conservation Area: 519-843-2979.

WEBSITE: www.grandriver.ca

The 47-km (29-mi) Elora Cataract Trailway crosses the Shand Dam and continues along the east side of Belwood Lake. Website: www.trailway.org

GRAND RIVER TAILWATER: FERGUS, ELORA, WEST MONTROSE

SPECIES: Brown trout, smallmouth bass, northern pike, carp, white sucker, bullhead, and yellow perch

Species	Jan	Feb	Mar	Apr	May	June	July	Aug	Sept	Oct	Nov	Dec
Brown Trout				•	*	*	*	•	*			
Pike					*	*	•	•	•	•	•	
Bass						•	•	•	•	•	•	
Carp				•	•	•	•	•	•			

FISHING HIGHLIGHTS: The Grand River tailwater is a world-renowned brown-trout fishery. It has healthy populations of this fish, as well as prolific insect hatches, and a local environment that has something for everyone. Anglers bring their fly rods from around the world to fish this easily accessed river, which is best done by wading. Canoes and other small boats are only appropriate in the lower tailwater area.

PUBLIC ACCESS: There are over twenty developed access sites along the Grand River tailwater. Belwood Lake Conservation Area and Elora Gorge Conservation Area are on this reach of river.

REGULATIONS: Special regulations apply in a good portion of this reach of river. These special regulations require anglers to use single barbless hooks; no organic bait is allowed, and anglers must release all trout.

The Grand River tailwater is one of the most easily accessible trout streams in North America.

FISHING THE GRAND RIVER TAILWATER

The Grand River tailwater is one of the most popular fishing areas of the Grand, and there is good reason for this. It is a world-class brown-trout fishery that has been called the best brown-trout tailwater in the east by many fly fishers. It is certainly a fine place to seek brown trout in beautiful surroundings. Add to this the other tourist amenities in the area and the incredible access to the river, and you do have a prime fishing destination that is sought after by anglers from around North America and the world.

The tailwater starts at the Shand Dam. This dam creates Belwood Lake Reservoir, one of the five major water-control structures on the Grand River. This large reservoir stores excess spring runoff to reduce flood damage and releases water in the dry months of summer to ensure a consistent water supply for downstream residents. This water is released largely from the middle and bottom portions of the reservoir, providing the river downstream with water colder than that on the surface of the reservoir. Trout and the insects they feed on find this a perfect habitat.

The Grand River tailwater near Elora, Ontario.

The "tailwater effect" influences the river downstream to about West Montrose. Local anglers and fisheries managers have identified three unique reaches to the tailwater. The upper tailwater is from the Shand Dam to Fergus. The middle reach extends from downtown Fergus through the Elora Gorge, and the lower tailwater runs from the low-level bridge at the downstream end of the gorge through to West Montrose. Each of these areas has its own unique character.

The upper tailwater is strongly influenced by the dam and its bedrock channel. This area has excellent hatches of caddis flies and midges, from both the river and the lake upstream, that help fish grow quickly. This is however, the most heavily fished area of the tailwater. Access points such as Belwood Lake Conservation Area, Second Line Garafraxa, Cedar Run, and the hydro lines are all excellent places to fish for brown trout. With a little walking, anglers can expect to have lots of space to fish, but you may encounter people upstream and downstream of you, especially on busy weekends in May and June.

To fool larger fish in this reach can require a stealthy approach, long leaders, and small flies attached to light tippets. Many of the fish in this area are fooled by "transitional flies," or emergers. However, there are times when the fish go on the feed and let their guard down. When this happens just about any fly in your box will produce good results. Caddis activity gets

The late Ted Knott with a Grand River tailwater brown trout.

going about the beginning of June and continues through the season.

The middle tailwater has more gravel and a more traditional riffle-pool structure. This results in more mayfly hatches and classic trout water areas. Cedar trees and limestone outcrops often frame the river. Even though much of the river flows through the towns of Fergus and Elora, it can feel as if you are in a wilderness area. The middle tailwater is a little less influenced by the dam, but it still benefits from the cool-water releases. Shading on the river in this area also helps to moderate temperatures. The tumbling riffles, deep pools, and boulder-studded runs provide a great variety of quality trout habitat. The scenic middle river is another popular area, but it does see fewer anglers than the upper stretch. The quality fish are also better distributed in the middle reach, as the habitat is more diverse.

Access to the middle tailwater usually requires going down a steep piece of riverbank. Stairs have been installed by Friends of the Grand volunteers with the help of the Ministry of Natural Resources at a couple of sites in this reach. Popular access points include Centennial Park in Fergus, the trails located near Angelica Street, the railway trestle on the rail trail between Fergus and Elora, and the Racket Ball Club just downstream of the trestle. Once anglers are in the river valley, walking along the riverbank or in the water can open up some beautiful places to fish. The Elora Gorge in this reach of river is a very scenic place to fish.

Good hatches in the middle tailwater begin in mid-May and continue through July. Some of the highlight hatches are the Hendricksons that usually occur near the end of May, the foxes, or March browns, that follow them in early June, and the Cahills that hatch throughout July. In addition to these larger mayflies, caddis are prolific in this area, and anglers will want to have a small yellow or cream-coloured cranefly imitation to fool picky fish. Smaller insects like BWOs, mahoganies, and tricos can be important through the spring and summer. Anglers can do very well with nymphing techniques and small pheasant-tail nymphs, hare's-ear nymphs, and caddis larvae. Sometimes sowbug imitations can be the hot ticket and, during the summer, crayfish patterns can excel. During overcast days or periods of low light, anglers pulling streamers can hook up with surprisingly large trout, bass, and pike.

For anglers with spinning tackle, a spinner with a barbless single hook or a small plug, again with a single barbless hook, can be effective. Since special regulations apply for most of the middle reach of the tailwater, bait or barbed hooks are not legal in much of this area. The areas of special regulation are usually well posted, but please check fishing regulations at www.mnr.gov.on.ca or pick up a copy of *2010 Ontario Recreational Fishing Regulations Summary* at a fishing-supply retailer in the area. Better yet, if you use only single barbless hooks, no bait, and release all trout, you can fish the entire tailwater reach without worry.

The valley becomes more open below the Elora Gorge. The river is easily accessed in the hamlet of Inverhaugh and at the public access of Wilson's Flats, at the twin bridges of Pilkington 8th Line. This is a transition area from a cold-water trout fishery to a warm-water fishery for bass. All anglers will enjoy the mixture of wily browns, northern pike, and scrappy smallmouth.

The scenic Grand River tailwater, near the rail-trail bridge between Fergus and Elora.

The lower tailwater is characterized by a wider, more gentle river channel. In the long pools and shallow riffles, you usually have more river to yourself. However, during certain times of the year, this area can be much more popular. During a good Hendrickson hatch in late May, you might not have an entire large pool to yourself as you usually will during the rest of the season. However, you will probably be focusing more on rising fish than on other anglers a couple of dozen metres or yards away! Generally, in the long, shallow pools of the lower tailwater, finding fish can be more of an issue than in upstream areas of the tailwater. They are there, they are just spread out more and better camouflaged.

The brown-trout density is not as high as areas upstream, but quality fish are certainly to be found in the lower tailwater. Fooling giant brown trout on long slick pools can be difficult, but it is incredibly rewarding for even the most seasoned fly angler. Most of the truly huge brown trout that are caught in the Grand each season come from this area. Popular places to access this reach of river include the Elora Gorge Trailer Park, Musselman's

Gate, Blondies, Wilson's Flats, and Townline Road.

Fishing in the Grand River tailwater varies with the season. Early in the trout season (late April and early May) the waters are much colder than in free-flowing streams. The influence of the dam keeps this water extra cold early in the season, and delays many insect hatches. This is a time when fishing with nymphs and streamers is most effective. The good old white woolly bugger and a caddis larvae imitation are the two most popular flies at this time, because they are incredibly successful.

The water warms more quickly as it gets farther from the dam. For this reason, hatches start in the lower tailwater before they do in the middle and upper reaches. Hendrickson mayflies usually start hatching in the second week of May near Wilson's Flats. This same hatch usually starts a week to ten days later near the railway trestle between Fergus and Elora. Other insects also hatch earlier lower down in the river. If you want to follow a hatch upstream, the bugs will still be in the middle reaches of the tailwater a couple of weeks later.

This warming trend continues later in the spring. By late June, the lower reaches of the tailwater are often warm enough in the middle of the day to decrease trout activity. During this time the fish can become nocturnal. You must fish at night, on overcast days, or very early in the morning, to find active fish in the lower tailwater. During this time, fish in the middle and upper reaches continue to feed throughout the day, since the water temperatures here are more comfortable for them.

By late July, warming daytime water temperatures also affect trout in the middle reach of the tailwater, and they become less active during the day. During late July through August, anglers are more concentrated in the upper reach of the tailwater, as this area offers the most active fish during the daytime, and good hatches of midges and caddis flies make for some excellent fishing.

During the heat of the summer through September, another factor can influence fishing. Algae coming from Belwood Lake can make the water a green-brown colour. If the algae is not too thick, this can result in excellent fishing, as it can help make your presentation stealthy. However, clumps of algae can also make fly presentations a bit more difficult. The farther downstream you go from the dam, the less the river is affected by the algae. Millions of caddis larvae take advantage of this concentrated food

Large brown trout attract anglers from around the world to the Grand River tailwater.

source and help filter it from the water.

This algae often coincides with what is called "summer turnover." This usually happens in late August, when the supply of cold water at the bottom of the reservoir is exhausted. The lake then mixes and warms from about 16° C to about 21° C in a couple of days. When this turnover occurs, it usually puts the fishing off for a few days until the fish acclimatize to the new water temperatures. At this time, cool nights reduce water temperatures, especially in the lower river. A few days after turnover, anglers who want to find active fish should start looking downstream.

These cool nights continue to improve the fishing through September. The last week or two of the season usually sees a flurry of activity in the search for big, beautiful, and aggressive brown trout.

The scenery of the Elora Gorge and the quaint towns that are already set up for tourists make this a great destination, especially for fly fishers. Catch-and-release regulations for about 75 per cent of the waters ensure that the river will always have a solid population of quality fish. A very conservative estimate of the financial contribution of this fishery has been calculated at well over a million dollars a year for the small communities of Fergus and Elora. This proves managing fisheries does pay!

RIVER FLOW LEVELS

The tailwater is directly influenced by the Shand Dam. This structure is designed to minimize flood damage in the spring and provide minimum flow-levels in summer to downstream communities. Normal summer flows from the Shand Dam are around 4.5 cm (1.5 in). Further downstream, below the Elora Gorge, normal summer flows are about 6 cm (2 in). The river is a joy to fish between 4 cm to 6 cm (1.5 to 2 in). In wet years, or if an extreme thunderstorm affects the area, water discharges may have to be increased at the dam. A warning siren is sounded if significant changes in water discharges are going to be made, and anglers should immediately vacate the area.

Heavy rains can also fill up the Irvine River, as it dumps into the Grand at the top of the Elora Gorge. This may make the lower tailwater unfishable, while the top portion remains unaffected. This is most common through the months of April and May, but it can happen at any time throughout the season. Flows of up to 10 cm (4 in) are still fishable. Flows above 10 cm (4 in) are tougher to fish, especially in the upper and middle reaches of the tailwater. Crossing the river can be difficult, and extreme care should be taken wading in these elevated flows. Above about 15 cms (530 cfs), the river's local guide services generally do not operate at any point on the river, and you should consider fishing in another area.

It is interesting that, when other rivers are in spate and unfishable due to high water levels, tailwater water levels are commonly good for fishing, especially in the upper and middle reaches. If there is storage capacity in the reservoir, release levels are often maintained at relatively normal flows or increased only slightly. To find out more about river flow in this area consult www.grandriver.ca.

GRAND RIVER TAILWATER HATCH CHART

Insect	Apr 1-30	May 1-15	May 16-31	June 1-15	June 16-30	July 1-15	July 16-31	Aug 1-15	Aug 16-31	Sept 1-15	Sept 16-30
BWO	*	*					*	*			*
Hendrickson			*	*							
March Brown				*							
Cahills					*	*	*				
Isonychia					*					*	
Mahogany					*	*					
Brown Drake				*							
Trico							*	*			
Hexagenia									*		
Cranefly				*	*	*	*	*	*		
Tan Caddis				*	*		*				*
Grey/Olive Caddis				*	*					*	*
Midges	*	*			*	*	*	*	*		

This chart identifies when these insects are active and when anglers may wish to use artificial flies to imitate them.

SIGHTS TO SEE: The Grand River Tailwater area is a popular destination for anglers, particularly because of the other attractions and amenities found in the area. The downtown areas of the villages of Fergus and

Mayfly hatches attract fly fishers to the Grand River tailwater.

Elora are built largely with local limestone. These downtown areas offer many interesting shops and boutiques that draw tourists year round. Local pubs and restaurants have their own unique local flavour, and these communities also have many top-quality B&Bs. The area's natural features are also part of the allure. The Lover's Leap, Tooth of Time, Templin Gardens, and the Elora Gorge are all must-sees for visitors. The historic 1881 West Montrose covered bridge is the last original covered bridge in Ontario, and the Elora Racetrack and Casino is a popular place to visit. The local landscape is dominated by prosperous farms, and there are several Mennonite farms where the farmers still use traditional horses and buggies for transportation. For fly fishers there is a specialty shop, Grand River Troutfitters, located right on the river in downtown Fergus (www.grandrivertroutfitters.com). There are also several other guiding services and fly-fishing stores on the Grand River in this area.

FOR MORE INFORMATION: visit www.ferguselora.com

Friends of the Grand River

Friends of the Grand River (FOGR) is a group of dedicated volunteers that is helping make the Grand River Tailwater a true world-class fishery. This group's 150 members do a lot of the unnoticed work that helps make the Grand River and Conestogo River Tailwater fisheries the success that they are today.

The group has helped develop and maintain over twenty access points to the Grand and Conestogo rivers with the help of its partners. Most of the safe parking areas and trails to the river have been built by FOGR volunteers. Annual road and river clean-ups to keep the area looking beautiful are part of FOGR's seasonal calendar. FOGR volunteers have also helped stock several hundred thousand brown trout in the rivers, bucket by bucket. This contributes significantly to the quality angling experience on the tailwaters.

This group's volunteers also help with education and enforcement on the river through their award-winning River Watch program, which helps local enforcement staff collect information and educate anglers about the special regulations in the area.

Grand Opportunities Fly Fishing Forum is another educational outlet that attracts fly anglers from around the province to learn more about fly fishing and the Grand River fishery. This event is held the first Saturday in June at Belwood Lake Conservation Area and has raised significant dollars to support research and environmental-improvement projects over the past several years.

The membership of FOGR has also conducted research projects to help better understand this unique fishery and, through tree-planting and in-river improvement projects, has contributed to improved water quality and fish habitat in the Grand, Conestogo, and several tributaries of these areas.

For more information or to get involved and become a Friend of the Grand visit www.friendsofthegrandriver.com.

ELORA GORGE CONSERVATION AREA

SPECIES: Brown trout, smallmouth bass, northern pike, carp

Species	Jan	Feb	Mar	Apr	May	June	July	Aug	Sept	Oct	Nov	Dec
Brown Trout				•	*	*	•	•	*			
Pike					•	•	•	•	•	•		
Bass						•	•	•	•	•		
Carp					•	•	•	•	•			

FISHING HIGHLIGHTS: Fly fishing in the 22-m (70-ft)-deep Elora Gorge provides some of the most scenic trout fishing in Canada for anglers who wade carefully. The river fishes very well through May and June and late September with a variety of insect hatches. In July and August fishing early or late in the day to take advantage of cooler temperatures is recommended. Spin fishing and fishing with bait are also quite effective in the gorge. The conservation area is open from the last Friday in April until the middle of October.

PUBLIC ACCESS: The GRCA owns 200 ha (500 ac) of land on both sides of the Grand River in the Elora Gorge Conservation Area. You can gain access to the river here from low areas such as the low-level bridge in the park. Park fees apply. Warning! Deep gorge! Stay back from the edge!

FISHING IN THE ELORA GORGE CONSERVATION AREA

The Grand River through the conservation area provides one of the most unique and diverse fishing opportunities in southern Ontario. The tight confines of the gorge present many heavy deep runs and pockets for anglers

The Elora Gorge is a scenic fishing location.

who wade carefully.

Within the park, fishing opportunities are excellent for wading anglers, with traditional riffle-pool stretches, plunge pools, and deep rock-lined runs. Care should be taken when wading on the slippery, moss-covered rocks in the gorge. A wading staff and/or cleats should be used.

Good flows for fishing in the gorge are up to 8 to 10 cm (283 to 353 cu ft) per second. Water levels in this stretch of the river can rise quickly after heavy rainfalls. In addition, the Irvine River can rise very rapidly after storms and increase flows in the gorge. The Irvine enters the Grand just below the Tooth of Time above the upstream edge of the conservation area. For current conditions call the River Information Line at 519-621-2763.

In the first few weeks of the season, large and aggressive browns are hungry for a big meal after a long winter. Drifting a large nymph through the deep pockets and runs will prove successful. This is an excellent time to cast big streamers such as woolly buggers, matukas, strip leeches, or crayfish patterns. Dead-drift these patterns through the deep pools or swing them through and hold on! Big, hungry browns can take flies very forcefully.

Through May and early June, the glassy pools of the gorge can provide excellent dry fly fishing with an abundance of hatching insects to imitate. But during the months of July and August, the fishing slows down as the "rubber hatch" comes into full swing. The gorge is a very popular area for tubing and, with the numbers of inner tubes floating by during the middle of the day, fishing can be difficult. At this time of year it is best to fish early and late when there are fewer tubers.

The gorge is not just a fly-fishing spot; spinning gear is also very effective. Spinners have long been the standards for fishing stream trout, and definitely should be used in the Grand. These flashy, erratic moving baits represent injured minnows and look like an easy meal for hungry browns. The best technique is to cast the spinner, quartering across the river, and slowly reel as the lure is swung downstream. Other popular lures include small minnow baits and small crankbaits, as well as small jigs in some of the deeper pools.

Anglers with live bait, flies, or jigs under a float can also have banner days fishing in the gorge. Some of the larger pools seem tailor-made for drifting bait through. Minnows, worms, and egg sacs are all solid choices for bait anglers. Fishing baits using bottom-bouncing techniques are tougher in the gorge. The number of large, erratic boulders that are found deep in runs and pools can grab a lot of tackle.

SIGHTS TO SEE: The gorge is a very scenic area that attracts visitors from around the world. Natural features include the Cascade Waterfall, Hole in the Rock, caves, and trails along the edge. The park features tubing down the Grand, a pond swimming area, and more than five hundred trailer and tent camping sites.

FOR MORE INFORMATION: phone 519-846-9742 or visit www.grandriver.ca

The nearby village of Elora's restaurants, pubs, shops, and boutiques are popular attractions, and, for those who enjoy the excitement of horse racing and slot machines, the Grand River Raceway is just across the street from the front gate of the Elora Gorge Conservation Area. Visit www.ferguselora.com

WEST MONTROSE TO BRIDGEPORT

SPECIES: Smallmouth bass, northern pike, carp, panfish

Species	Jan	Feb	Mar	Apr	May	June	July	Aug	Sept	Oct	Nov	Dec
Bass					*	*	*	•	•			
Pike	•	•	•		*	*	•	•	•	•		
Carp				•	•	•	•	•	•	•		
Panfish				•	•	•	•	•	•	•		

FISHING HIGHLIGHTS: There are some good fishing areas for shorebound or wading anglers in this reach of river. But to experience the best fishing, a canoe or other small boat is really helpful. The smallmouth bass fishing is most popular, but many urban anglers target pike and carp in the deeper pools that are found as the Grand River winds through Kitchener–Waterloo. The spring pike fishing can be good.

PUBLIC ACCESS: Several trails and landings are found in the K–W area. Winterborne Bridge, RIM Park Trail, Priddle Park in Conestogo, and Kaufmann Flats in Waterloo are all good canoe or wading access points. There is shore-fishing access at Bridgeport.

FISHING THE GRAND RIVER FROM WEST MONTROSE TO BRIDGEPORT

This stretch of river is known for its smallmouth fishing, and for good pike fishing in the spring. A popular way to fish the river is to float it in a canoe, stopping at various points to fish deeper pools or runs. With a canoe you can cover a lot of water and fish the best spots. There are countless access

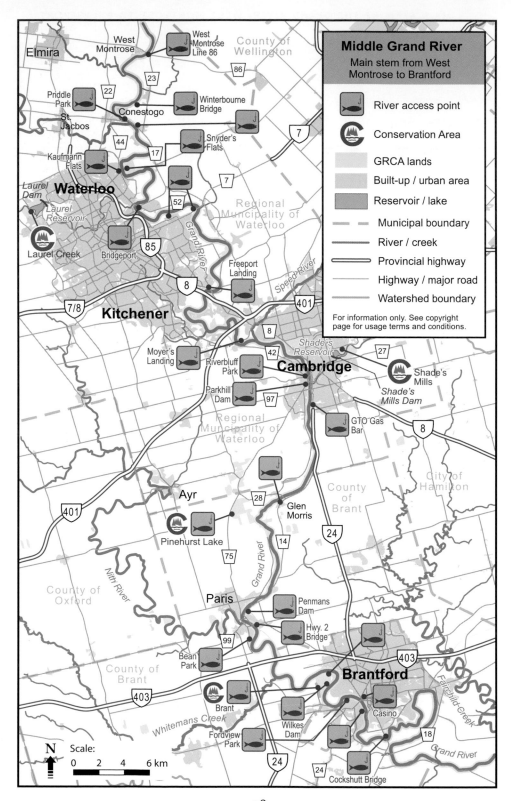

Middle Grand River

Main stem from West Montrose to Brantford

- 🐟 River access point
- 🅖 Conservation Area
- GRCA lands
- Built-up / urban area
- Reservoir / lake
- — — Municipal boundary
- —— River / creek
- ═══ Provincial highway
- —— Highway / major road
- —— Watershed boundary

For information only. See copyright page for usage terms and conditions.

Elmira

West Montrose

West Montrose Line 86

County of Wellington

23

86

Priddle Park

22

Winterbourne Bridge

Conestogo

7

St. Jacobs

44

Snyder's Flats

17

Kaufmann Flats

7

Laurel Dam

Waterloo

52

Laurel Reservoir

Regional Municipality of Waterloo

Grand River

Laurel Creek

Bridgeport

85

Freeport Landing

Speed River

8

401

7/8

Kitchener

8

Moyer's Landing

42

Shade's Reservoir

27

Riverbluff Park

Cambridge

Shade's Mills

Parkhill Dam

97

Shade's Mills Dam

GTO Gas Bar

8

Regional Municipality of Waterloo

401

Ayr

28

Glen Morris

County of Brant

City of Hamilton

Pinehurst Lake

14

24

75

County of Oxford

Nith River

Grand River

Paris

Penmans Dam

Hwy. 2 Bridge

403

99

Bean Park

Brantford

County of Brant

403

Brant

Wilkes Dam

Casino

Whitemans Creek

Fordview Park

18

Fairchild Creek

Grand River

N

Scale:

0 2 4 6 km

24

24

Cockshutt Bridge

The covered bridge in West Montrose is the last of its kind in Ontario.

points for wading anglers in this stretch of river, but please respect private property and ask permission to enter private land.

This stretch of the Grand is known for pike fishing from January 1 to March 31, and from the opener in mid-May to December 31. In May, pike are very aggressive, as they have just finished spawning and are feeding heavily to regain weight. Casting brightly coloured spinnerbaits, crankbaits in a variety of colours, and even topwater lures, can be very effective. If fish do not respond to bright lures, switch over to slow-moving baits, such as a big white or yellow twist-tail grub or live bait. Even sluggish pike find it difficult to refuse a lively minnow drifted through a deep hole below a float.

It is important to note that smallmouth bass are spawning at this time of the year. Release any bass immediately if you catch one accidentally. It is illegal to fish for bass until the season opens on the last Saturday in June.

By the end of June the smallmouth have finished spawning and moved into the deep pools and runs to feed. The most spectacular time to fish for smallmouth at this time of the year is at dawn or dusk.

These periods of low light offer the chance to use topwater baits, such as stickbaits and poppers, and swimming frog imitations, preferably over the surface of pools. When the topwater action begins to fade, it's time to switch over to baits that get to the bottom of the river. Tube jigs and grubs are the best choice to comb the bottom of a pool for bigger smallmouths. Use colours that include smoke, brown, white, and other natural colours. Small, medium, and deep-diving crankbaits in a variety of colours can also produce. Never overlook a spinnerbait which can be used at a variety of depths. Chartreuse is the favourite colour locally, but white, black, and other colours can also produce good results.

For fly fishers, working a topwater fly (Dalhberg diver, deer-hair popper) over a deep pool is a great way to tempt a big smallmouth to explode on your bait. If the bass will not come to the surface for your fly, switch to sub-surface patterns, such as streamers, crayfish patterns, and woolly buggers, to work the depths of pools and runs. Nymph fishing with large buggy-looking nymphs, crayfish imitations, or woolly buggers in areas with current, depth, and scattered boulders can be very productive too, and areas like this should not be overlooked.

As river temperatures cool in the fall, smallmouth start moving to the deepest pools and feeding heavily in preparation for the long winter. You may have to work to find the fish, but, when you do, you usually find them concentrated in a small area. Deep, slow presentations in the fall are usually the most effective. Tubes and grubs excel at pulling fish from deep pools. Autumn also provides an excellent opportunity for fly fishers looking for action after the trout season closes at the end of September. Streamers, woolly buggers, and crayfish patterns will account for most of the fish caught at this time of the year. A good tip is to use large, weighted flies that can get down into a deep pool and look tasty to a big bronzeback. As a conservation practice, in the fall please limit your harvest. Highly concentrated fish are very susceptible to over-fishing, and taking too many can affect the river for a number of years, since river bass are very slow-growing fish.

WATER LEVELS: Normal low summer flow for the Grand River from West Montrose to the Conestogo confluence is 6.5 cms (230 cfs). The river can still fish quite well up to about 20 cm (8 in). For current levels, phone the River Information Line at 519-621-2763 or check online at www.grandriver.ca.

The Grand at West Montrose.

SIGHTS TO SEE: Gently rolling countryside and fine views make this an attractive area to tour. Here the Grand River is lined by farms and heritage homes. The only remaining original wooden covered bridge in Ontario crosses the Grand River at West Montrose. The Grand Valley Hiking Trail also runs close to the river. The Grand can provide a wilderness feel in an urban area. As the river flows into Kitchener–Waterloo it still has a very natural shoreline. Area attractions include historic sites and homes, art galleries and museums, outlet shopping, the St. Jacobs farmers' market, and a wide range of accommodations and restaurants.

FOR MORE INFORMATION: Waterloo Region Tourism at 877-585-7517 or www.explorewaterlooregion.com
   St. Jacobs Country at www.stjacobs.com or 1-800-265-3353
   Woolwich Township tourism www.woolwich.ca or 519-669-6000

SNYDER'S FLATS, BLOOMINGDALE

This restored gravel pit area can be accessed off the Snyder's Flats Road in Bloomingdale, right across the river from RIM Park in Waterloo. Walk in from the parking area and gate. The three ponds are home to largemouth bass, smallmouth bass, carp, sunfish, northern pike, and crappie. Most of the shoreline can be productive. Fishing with bait and a bobber is often effective, and working the water with various lures and soft plastic baits can result in a good number of hookups.

Fishing for crappie at Snyder's Flats.

KITCHENER–WATERLOO TO CAMBRIDGE

SPECIES: Smallmouth bass, pike, carp, black crappie, panfish, redhorse suckers

Species	Jan	Feb	Mar	Apr	May	June	July	Aug	Sept	Oct	Nov	Dec
Bass						*	*	*	*	•		
Pike					•	•	•	•	•	•		
Carp				•	*	*	*	•	•	•		
Panfish				*	*	*	•	•	•	•		

FISHING HIGHLIGHTS: Fishing is surprisingly good in this highly urbanized section of the Grand River. Look for spring crappies in slow-water areas and around structures just above the Parkhill Dam in Cambridge. Summer produces excellent smallmouth fishing from the Parkhill Dam upstream to the Galt Country Club. Some pike-fishing opportunities exist in the spring, although this is not a top pike-fishing area.

PUBLIC ACCESS: Freeport Landing in Kitchener, Moyer's Blair Landing, Riverbluff Park, Parkhill Bridge, and the GTO Gas Station access on Highway #24 in Cambridge are all excellent places to launch canoes or access the river by wading. There is also access at all bridge crossings in this area, and there are several riverside parks and trails leading to the river. The Walter Bean Grand River Trail can be especially useful for anglers on foot or bicycle.

Evening bass fishing near Kitchener.

FISHING THE GRAND FROM KITCHENER–WATERLOO TO CAMBRIDGE

This stretch of the river is popular with youngsters because it is within biking distance of town.

Pike fishing is not as good here as it is elsewhere on the Grand, but you can still find some action in the spring, when pike are aggressive and hungry. If bold and bright presentations are not producing, try switching to slow-moving baits, such as a big white or yellow twist-tail grub or live bait. The best areas to fish are around the deep holes, but pike can be found almost anywhere.

Spring in southern Ontario is associated with panfishing, and the river just above the Mannheim Weir in Kitchener and the Parkhill Dam in Cambridge are known locally for a booming crappie population. Look for crappies around areas of slower water or along any rip-rap or man-made structure. Crappies tend to swim in small groups, and once you find one, you will likely find more. The best tactics for these tasty fish are to use small tube jigs and grubs or a minnow below a float.

Parkhill Dam in downtown Cambridge.

In the heart of Cambridge, anglers can expect to find smallmouth bass, rock bass, carp, and suckers willing to be presented a bait. Powerboats can be launched above the Parkhill Dam to fish upstream as far as the Galt Country Club. A good area for smallmouth is around the old train-trestle footing, where broken boulders and rip-rap along the shore provide some structure. Use grubs and tubes for smallmouth through this area. Below the Parkhill Dam, you can launch a canoe and paddle and fish all the way to Paris before you have to portage again.

Fall fishing tips for this area are also very much the same as those mentioned in the previous Kitchener–Waterloo section. Here the fall colours add a special dimension as you reach the northern edge of the Carolinian forest just below Cambridge. Look for smallmouth in deep pools and use tubes and grubs. Fly fishers should try streamers and crayfish patterns.

BEWARE OF DAMS IN THIS AREA

The Parkhill Road dam, Cambridge, and the Mannheim Water Treatment Plant dam in Kitchener are dangerous places for anglers and canoeists. Watch for buoys and canoe portages above the dams, and stay clear of the "boil," or deadly undertow, below the dams. Normal low summer flow for the Grand River between the Conestogo confluence above Kitchener and the Speed River confluence in Cambridge is 11 cms (388 cfs). Higher flows make the dams even more dangerous. Current river levels can be obtained from the River Information Line at 519-621-2763 or online at www.grandriver.ca.

SIGHTS TO SEE: The area is rich with scenic riverbank trails, heritage architecture, and special events, such as Cambridge Riverfest in the first weekend in June. Nearby attractions include the Doon Heritage Crossroads; Bingeman's Amusement Park and Conference Centre; historic sites and homes; art galleries and museums; Southworks factory outlets; art galleries; restaurants for every budget; the Cambridge–Paris Trailhead; and the African Lion Safari.

FOR MORE INFORMATION: Cambridge Visitor and Convention Bureau 800-749-7560 or 519-653-1424, or Waterloo Region Tourism at 519-585-7517.
Grand River Country at 866-900-4722 or www.grandrivercountry.com

CAMBRIDGE TO PARIS

SPECIES: Smallmouth bass, pike, crappie, carp, sunfish, rock bass, redhorse suckers, and walleye.

Species	Jan	Feb	Mar	Apr	May	June	July	Aug	Sept	Oct	Nov	Dec
Bass						*	*	*	*	•		
Pike	•	•	*		*	•	•	•	•	•		
Carp				•	*	*	*	•	•			

FISHING HIGHLIGHTS: This is a very popular area for canoe trippers. Taking a fishing rod along can reward anglers with good catches of smallmouth bass. This stretch of the river includes small rapids, riffles, and deeper holes. The river widens upstream of Penman's Dam in Paris, where a variety of fish can be found.

PUBLIC ACCESS: The best access points are the canoe launch-load sites at the GTO station on Highway #24 in south Cambridge. The Cambridge to Paris Rail-Trail parallels the river, making access easy. Two other access locations are Washington Street in Glen Morris and above the dam off Willow Street in Paris.

FISHING THE GRAND, CAMBRIDGE TO PARIS

This area is a very popular canoe route, because it combines beautiful scenery with an easily accessible and "user-friendly" river. The Grand has enough easy whitewater to provide some challenge and a lot of relatively flat-moving water to make paddling a few kilometres easy. Canoeists should take particular care when water levels are high and fast in the spring or after a very heavy rainfall. If flows are high, watch for whitewater and standing waves in the small rapids south of Glen Morris.

Anglers often fish from a canoe, or get out near deeper holes to work

The Penman's Dam in Paris is a Grand River landmark.

productive waters. A great way to spend a summer day is to canoe down-river, floating and fishing where areas look promising.

This is one of the best stretches of the river for bass fly angling, using top-water flies like Dahlberg divers and small poppers. For sub-surface fishing, try woolly buggers, small minnow patterns, buggy nymphs, and crayfish imitations. If one doesn't work, try another until you match what the fish are feeding on that day.

Although pike are not as prolific in this stretch of river as in other reaches of the Grand, spring fishing can produce good results, especially in the deep holes along the river. Anglers should look for pike in the quiet waters below a riffle. The deep water upstream of the Paris dam is also a good place to seek out pike in the spring.

In the fall, anglers can enjoy both good uncrowded fishing and

These stately abandoned railway bridge piers are a landmark just upstream of Paris.

spectacular fall colours along the riverbanks. Smallmouth fishing is excellent, using tube jigs, grubs, and spinners. Fish tend to congregate as they look for wintering areas, and you might have to work one or two spots to find them. It is not uncommon to find twenty or thirty aggressively feeding fish at the right hole. Please limit your harvest when you find a pod of big aggressive fish, as smallmouth grow slowly and are very vulnerable to overharvest at this time of year. The future of the river's fishery is in your hands.

Fly fishers will be right at home using streamers and poppers for the aggressive bass found in this reach of the Grand. Slowing down and fishing deeper holes with a nymph rig and a big woolly bugger or a crayfish or nymph imitation can hook you up with some really nice bass and the occasional carp.

WATER LEVELS: Normal summer flows in the Grand River from the Speed River confluence in Cambridge to the Nith River confluence in Paris are in the 15-cms range (530 cfs). If you fish near Penman's Dam in Paris, stay clear of the "boil," or deadly undertow, below the dam. Contact the River Information Line at 519-621-2763 or www.grandriver.ca.

SIGHTS TO SEE: This very scenic stretch of the Grand River flows through a forested valley with little sign of urbanization. It is a popular area for canoeists, rafters, and hikers. A canoe portage has been built around Penman's Dam in Paris, and public washrooms are provided at the nearby arena. For hikers and cyclists, the Cambridge to Paris Rail-Trail follows the Grand River for 19 km (11 mi) from Cambridge to Paris and then on an additional 60 km (37 mi) to Brantford and Hamilton, with several access points and parking lots en route. The Town of Paris includes attractive heritage architecture, town parks on the Grand and the Nith rivers, a fine linen shop, riverside restaurants, and boutique shopping.

FOR MORE INFORMATION: Town of Paris/County of Brant 519-442-6324. or www.brant.ca

Grand River Country at 866-900-4722 or www.grandrivercountry.com

PINEHURST LAKE CONSERVATION AREA

SPECIES: Smallmouth bass, largemouth bass, sunfish, yellow perch

Species	Jan	Feb	Mar	Apr	May	June	July	Aug	Sept	Oct	Nov	Dec
Bass						*	•	•	*	*		
Sunfish					•							

FISHING HIGHLIGHTS: Located west of the main Grand River just north of Paris, this kettle lake is worth mention, and is a perfect place to introduce a youngster to fishing. It is easily accessible, and the overabundant small sunfish will cooperate with a simple setup that includes a float, a small hook, and a piece of a worm.

PUBLIC ACCESS: The GRCA owns 140 ha (450 ac) of land at Pinehurst, including a 9-ha (23-ac) spring-fed kettle lake with one boat launch. No powerboats are allowed, but canoe and paddleboat rentals are available. Pinehurst is open from the last Friday in April until the middle of October. Pinehurst Lake Conservation Area is located halfway between Cambridge and Paris on Highway #24A or Regional Road #75, and roughly halfway between highways #401 and #403.

FISHING AT PINEHURST LAKE CONSERVATION AREA

Pinehurst Lake was scooped out by ice during the last period of glaciation. It is fed by underground springs, with no surface streams entering the lake. As a result there is no surface runoff to the lake, and the water quality is quite high. The lake is 10 m (35 ft) at its deepest point.

Pinehurst is the place where families can have fun for a day, fishing

Fishing is a family experience at Pinehurst Lake.

for largemouth bass, crappie, and bluegill. Try topwater lures, crankbaits, jerkbaits, rubber worms, and spinnerbaits. Twistertail jigs are also good all-purpose lures for this area. This lake is home to an overabundance of small sunfish, which makes this a perfect location to introduce someone to fishing. These fish are common and usually hungry. Keeping things simple is usually the best way to go. A small hook, a split shot, and piece of worm suspended under a small float will attract the attention of hungry panfish. If you wish to use artificial lures, try small jigs under the float and tiny spinners and minnow baits. The new scented plastic baits in tiny sizes are especially effective at keeping the kids busy with the bluegills of Pinehurst.

Fly fishers using small topwater baits such as grasshoppers and poppers will have lots of action, and below the surface small nymphs and streamers should keep you busy with the abundant sunfish and small bass found in Pinehurst Lake. It is a good training ground for those intending to try for bigger fish in other areas.

Plans are in the works to add a top predator to this system to help get the fish population into a better balance, in which there are fewer but larger panfish and a healthy population of predators that use the sunfish as a food source. When this happens, the fishery at Pinehurst may change and offer anglers a better chance to hook up with quality fish. This lake does have a healthy growth of aquatic vegetation and excellent cover that should support quality fish like largemouth bass and either pike or musky.

SIGHTS TO SEE: Lush Carolinian forest covers most of this area. Nearby attractions include the F. W. R. Dickson Wilderness Area, a five-minute drive to the Cambridge to Paris Rail-Trail, the Town of Paris, the City of Cambridge, and canoe access to the Grand River.

At Pinehurst Lake Conservation Area, three hundred serviced and unserviced campsites are provided, with computerized reservations, a volleyball court, a baseball diamond, canoe rentals, and 12 km (7 mi) of hiking trails. The park features snowshoeing and ice fishing in winter.

FOR MORE INFORMATION: Pinehurst Lake Conservation Area at 519-442-4721 or www.grandriver.ca

PARIS TO BRANTFORD: GRAND RIVER EXCEPTIONAL WATERS

SPECIES: Smallmouth bass, rainbow trout, brown trout, walleye, channel catfish, black crappie, carp, redhorse suckers, panfish

Species	Jan	Feb	Mar	Apr	May	June	July	Aug	Sept	Oct	Nov	Dec
Small-mouth bass						*	*	*	*	•		
Rainbow Trout				•	•	•			•	*	*	•
Carp				•	*	*	*	•	•	•		
Walleye					•	•	•	•	*	*	•	

FISHING HIGHLIGHTS: The Exceptional Waters area has a special fishery that has been identified by many anglers. The rainbow trout fishing in the fall can be exceptional, and the smallmouth bass fishing in the summer is also excellent. To protect these special fisheries there are no-kill regulations that apply to a significant portion of this area. The water provides great fishing for wading anglers and people who fish the river by canoe or drift boat.

PUBLIC ACCESS: Boat anglers will make use of launch and load sites in Paris at Bean Park, Brant Conservation Area, D'Aubigny Park, and Cockshutt Bridge off Erie Avenue in Brantford. Shore-bound and wading anglers frequently use the following: Bean Park, Downtown Paris, Highway #403; Brant Park; Wilkes Dam; Waterworks Park; D'Aubigny Park; Fordview Park; Brantford Casino; and Lions Park trail and the Gordon Glaves Memorial Pathway trails that run along the river in this area.

SPECIAL REGULATIONS: Special Regulations apply to a portion of the river from the Highway #2 bridge in Paris through to the

75

pedestrian bridge above Wilkes Dam in Brantford. No organic bait can be used, only single barbless hooks are allowed, and anglers must release all fish.

Extended regulations for rainbow trout allow fishing for this species from 100 m downstream of the Highway #2 bridge in Paris to the edge of Lake Erie, from the fourth Saturday in April to the end of December.

FISHING FROM PARIS TO BRANTFORD

Anglers who enjoy beautiful scenery and fishing for rainbow trout and smallmouth bass in a river setting will be drawn to the Exceptional Waters Area of the Grand River.

This reach is close to the major population centres of Brantford, Cambridge, and Hamilton, and is attracting a lot of attention among anglers. A stretch of special interest is found between Paris and Brantford. In this reach there is a section of river that has been designated catch-and-release for all species, bass included. The results of this "let 'em go" regulation is that more bass have a chance to grow and reproduce. Expect to find large numbers of good-sized bass in this area for a long time to come.

There is limited shore access in this reach of river, though wading anglers can get into some good fishing. Nevertheless, to really experience what this area is all about, a canoe or drift boat is the way to go. There are several businesses that can help you with canoe rentals, vehicle shuttles, and guided drift boats. There is a thriving smallmouth-bass population, resident and migratory rainbow trout, and even a few walleye.

Bass thrive in the river's deep runs, boulder-studded pools, and large and productive riffles. The habitat in this reach of river is excellent for this feisty species. They enjoy eating a variety of foods that can be imitated with a wide assortment of lures and flies. Pick your favourite technique and hold on. The water in this reach is usually quite clear, so natural baits get the nod here versus gaudy colours, but let the fish decide what they want to bite on any given day.

The Exceptional Waters reach is also an area that is growing in popularity for people who are fly-fishing for migratory rainbow trout or steelhead. Fly rods are a common sight at popular runs throughout the fall extended season. Many anglers use double-handed, or Spey, rods in this area. These longer

This fly fisher is enjoying the Exceptional Waters between Paris and Brantford.

rods are often 4 to 4.5 m (13 to 15 ft) long, and allow anglers to cover more water and show flies to more fish using a "traditional" down-and-across swinging technique. Large black, purple, or orange flies are common, and some anglers combine these hot colours into the same pattern. Flies with flowing materials that provide a lot of fish-attracting movement are better producers than stiff and lifeless patterns. Various Spey patterns, rabbit strip leeches, and woolly bugger variations are most commonly used by successful anglers. In lower and clearer waters, more subtle flies are often used with great success.

Catch-and-release regulations for all fish species in a portion of the Exceptional Waters are making this a great place to enjoy some fantastic fishing. In the first few years after the regulations were put in place, there was already a noticeable improvement in the numbers and size of smallmouth bass in the catch-and-release area.

Bait fishing is not allowed in the waters from the Highway #2 bridge in

Trophy smallmouth bass like this can be over 20 years old.

Paris to the pedestrian bridge in Brantford. In this part of the Exceptional Waters, spinning and float-fishing tackle are allowed, provided anglers use artificial lures or flies and a single barbless hook. A silver spinner can be very productive. Waters downstream of the pedestrian bridge in Brantford are covered by standard provincial regulations, and baits like egg sacs are legal and quite productive.

The rainbows that have navigated the dams in Dunnville, Caledonia, and Brantford are big, strong, and aggressive when they reach the waters between Paris and Brantford, offering anglers one of the greatest challenges in the Grand River. These fish are migratory, so they are not always easy to

Canoeing is a popular way to access the fishing in the Exceptional Waters area.

find, but when you do hook up, expect a memorable experience.

Popular areas for rainbow anglers are the Westcast Rapid off Powerline Road, at the mouth of Whitemans Creek, above and below Wilkes Dam, in downtown Brantford at Oak Hill Cemetery, D'Aubigny Park and Fordview Park, and near Cockshutt Bridge.

FISHING IN DOWNTOWN PARIS

In the town of Paris, the river is accessible by wading anglers and canoeists. The deep pockets in the river are home to smallmouth bass, carp, and rock bass. Wading the river right in town during summer flows is a great way to spend an afternoon with a light spinning outfit or a fly rod. Below the dam in Paris and at the mouth of the Nith River are prime spots to get hooked up with one of the numerous smallmouth bass that call this area home. The Grand River below Penman's Dam in Paris is a mixture of riffles and pools, bounded by a wide valley of mature trees and farmland.

D'Aubigny Creek

D'Aubigny Creek, a small stream that runs through a rapidly urbanizing area in the City of Brantford, is not unlike the dozens of other urban streams in the watershed, except that a local school has adopted this creek and is continually improving it. The students at Pauline Johnson Secondary School are using D'Aubigny Creek as a classroom to teach biology lessons and life lessons in caring for the environment. The students are led by teacher Tom Sitak and volunteers from the Brantford Steelheaders in a variety of lessons that go beyond measuring the surface area of the creek, identifying aquatic invertebrates, and rolling a few rocks. The greater goal is building environmental leaders of tomorrow through hands-on action — literally in their own backyards.

Floating Paris to Brantford

Bean Park in Paris is a perfect place to embark on a float trip down the river. Floating the river opens up a lot of opportunities to fish the long pools and deep runs that are a challenge to reach from shore. A canoe or a Mackenzie-style drift boat are ideal for fishing the Grand from Bean Park down to Brant Park. This entire reach provides exceptional habitat for smallmouth bass, and fishing during the heat of summer can be excellent. Early in the spring and through the fall, anglers can expect to find rainbow trout, and the occasional brown trout, scattered throughout the area, especially downstream of Whitemans Creek.

Catch-and-release regulations for all species of fish apply in this stretch of river from the put-in point in Paris to the pedestrian bridge in Brantford just a couple hundred metres or yards above the take-out at Brant Park. This is an exceptional place to enjoy some fantastic fishing. In the first few years since the regulations were implemented, there is already a noticeable improvement in the numbers and size of smallmouth bass.

This reach of river has numerous large riffles and deep runs that provide perfect habitat for bass and trout. Anglers will also encounter healthy

Fishing and canoeing between Paris and Brantford.

populations of carp and redhorse suckers.

The mouth of Whitemans Creek often contains brown trout and rainbow trout that are either migrating through or taking advantage of the prolific insect hatches found in this part of the river. Through the fall, anglers try for migrating fish that hold in the main river below the creek, and some rainbow trout feed on the flat below Whitemans Creek down to Wilkes Dam through the spring and early summer. This is a great place to fly-fish if you enjoy making long casts to rising rainbows.

The deep water above Wilkes Dam conceals some remnants of older dams, and some deep holes that provide quality habitat for a variety of fish. Here you can find resident smallmouth bass, walleye, and rainbow trout during their migration period. Pike and brown trout add to the diverse fishery in this area.

The Grand River flows past Brant Park Conservation Area immediately before entering the City of Brantford. At the lower end of Brant Park, the Wilkes Dam necessitates a portage for canoeists.

The river is a good size below the 403 bridge near Brantford.

FLOATING BRANT PARK TO COCKSHUTT BRIDGE

This part of the river has much deeper holes than the reach from Paris to Brantford. Due to its depth, weed growth is less of an issue than it can be between Paris and Brantford during the late summer and early fall. The deep waters in this reach are home to walleye, pike, and bass. There is also quality water closer to the Cockshutt Bridge and good places to target bass and steelhead in season. This reach provides a great place to enjoy a half or full day's fishing.

WATER LEVELS: Normal low summer flows in the Grand River from the Nith River confluence in Paris to Lake Erie are 19 cms (671 cfs). For current water levels call the River Information Line at 519-621-2763.

SIGHTS TO SEE: In Brantford, attractions include: floral gardens and attractive trails throughout the city; historic architecture; the Woodland Cultural Centre; Brantford Riverfest on the last weekend in May; the Bell Homestead, where the first long-distance phone call was placed; the Brantford Charity Casino, along the banks of the river in downtown Brantford; a variety of shops and boutiques; the Wayne Gretzky Sports Centre; the Sanderson Centre for the Performing Arts; and Her Majesty's Royal Chapel of the Mohawks.

FOR MORE INFORMATION: Tourism Brantford at 800-265-6299 or www.visitbrantford.ca

Grand River Country 866-900-4722 or www.grandrivercountry.com

Exceptional Waters Continues to Flourish

Some areas of the Grand are truly "exceptional." In fact, one of these areas has even been officially designated as "Exceptional Waters." The reach of river from Paris to Brantford has scenic beauty, diverse history, super fishing opportunities, and a committee from the local community that is protecting and promoting the area and striving to improve and maintain its value.

The Exceptional Waters Community Advisory Committee partners have helped build river-access sites like Bean Park in Paris, as well as Brant Park and Cockshutt Bridge in Brantford. These sites now have safe parking, information kiosks, garbage receptacles, and areas suitable to launch or load small boats and canoes. In addition, several directional signs have been put up in key places to help residents and visitors find these access locations.

Volunteers have been monitoring the health of the river by taking invertebrate samples at selected locations over the past few years. Following the populations of these bugs will help determine water-quality changes over time. At this point, the populations seem to be abundant and diverse, indicating a high-quality aquatic environment. Volunteers also participate in the local "Eagle Watch" program. An increasing number of bald eagles are using this area as a wintering and nesting area, and volunteers are documenting the comeback of this majestic bird.

With improved awareness of the special resources found in the Exceptional Waters area, there is an increase in the number of groups that are helping with cleanup activities. Each year there are several road and river cleanup events supported by business, school groups, and volunteer partners. With continued community support, the Exceptional Waters area of the Grand River should remain a destination for visitors and a place to be proud of in the local community.

BRANT CONSERVATION AREA

SPECIES: Smallmouth bass, rainbow trout, northern pike, walleye, bullhead, carp

Species	Jan	Feb	Mar	Apr	May	June	July	Aug	Sept	Oct	Nov	Dec
Bass						*	•	•	*	*		
Rainbow Trout				*	*	•			•	*	*	•
Pike					•	•	•	•	•	•		
Carp				•	*	*	*	•	•	•		
Walleye					•	•	•	•	•	•	•	

FISHING HIGHLIGHTS: Anglers can fish above and below Wilkes Dam from Brant Conservation Area. Fishing from shore and by boat are all possible and productive at this park, as is wading. Rainbow trout and smallmouth bass are most sought after in this area, but many more species are caught regularly.

PUBLIC ACCESS: The Brant Conservation Area is located on Jennings Road, on the west side of Brantford (and the west bank of the Grand River). Take Highway #53 west to Oakhill Drive, then go north on Oakhill and right onto Jennings Road. By river, it is 8 km (5 mi) downstream of Paris. The GRCA owns 185 ha (456 ac) of land in the oxbow formed by the Grand River on the west edge of Brantford. There are many river access areas in the Brant Conservation Area and a gravel boat launch is located within the park. A portage goes around Wilkes Dam on the east bank, and another launch area is located downstream of Wilkes Dam. Entrance fees apply. The park is open from the last Friday

Fishing downstream of the Wilkes Dam at Brant Conservation Area.

in April until the middle of October. The swimming pool opens in early June and closes on Labour Day.

FISHING BRANT CONSERVATION AREA

From Brant Park anglers can fish above and below Wilkes Dam. Above the dam is a deep-water pool while below is a fast-flowing river with riffles, runs, and deep holes.

The river below the dam is home to smallmouth bass, mooneye, walleye, and migratory rainbow trout. This water is best accessed by wading. Care should be taken around the dam area and in higher flows. Make sure to check the GRCA's flow data to see if river levels are safe before heading out.

In the deep water above the dam, the diverse habitat of deep holes and structure afforded by rubble and remnants of an old dam provide a variety of fishing opportunities. Here smallmouth and walleye can be found, as well as pike and rainbow trout. This deep water extends up to the pedestrian

Spey Clave instructor Andy Murray fishing near Brant Park.

bridge. A small boat or canoe is an excellent way to reach this water to cast or troll for a diversity of fish.

WATER LEVELS: Average summer low flows in this stretch of the river are 19 cms (318 cfs), though water levels can rise slowly after periods of heavy rain. Before Brant Park opens in the spring, much of it is occasionally flooded by the Grand. If you fish near the Wilkes Dam on the edge of the park, stay away from the dam and clear of the "boil," or deadly undertow, below the dam. For current river conditions, call the River Information Line at 519-621-2763 or www.grandriver.ca.

SIGHTS TO SEE: Brant Conservation Area provides 400 serviced and unserviced campsites, with computerized reservations, showers, a 0.6-ha (1.5-ac) swimming pool, playgrounds, canoe rentals, picnic areas and shelters, a baseball diamond, and a Visitor Services program.

FOR MORE INFORMATION: Call Brant Conservation Area at 519-752-2040 or visit www.grandriver.ca.

BRANTFORD TO CALEDONIA

SPECIES: Smallmouth bass, walleye, black crappie, white crappie, mooneye, redhorse suckers, freshwater drum, northern pike, carp, panfish

Species	Jan	Feb	Mar	Apr	May	June	July	Aug	Sept	Oct	Nov	Dec
Bass						*	*	*	*	•	•	
Pike	•	•	*		*	•	•	•	•	•		
Walleye				•	•	•	•	•	•	•	•	
Carp				•	•	•	•	•	•			
Crappie			*	*	•	•	•	•	•	•	*	*

FISHING HIGHLIGHTS: There are diverse types of fishing to target in this area throughout the season. Anglers should look for creek mouths, riverbend pools, weed lines, bridges, and sunken islands to find the greatest fish concentrations. The deeper, slower-moving waters of this section of the Grand River are also popular with powerboaters.

PUBLIC ACCESS: The river can be accessed at boat launches located at Chiefswood Trailer Park at Ohsweken, and Lafortune Park north of Caledonia. The west bank of the river from just south of Brantford to Caledonia is part of the Six Nations Reserve. Permission must be obtained from the landowner before entering private property. Highway #54 south follows the Grand River from Brantford to Caledonia. From Hamilton, Caledonia can be reached by Highway #6.

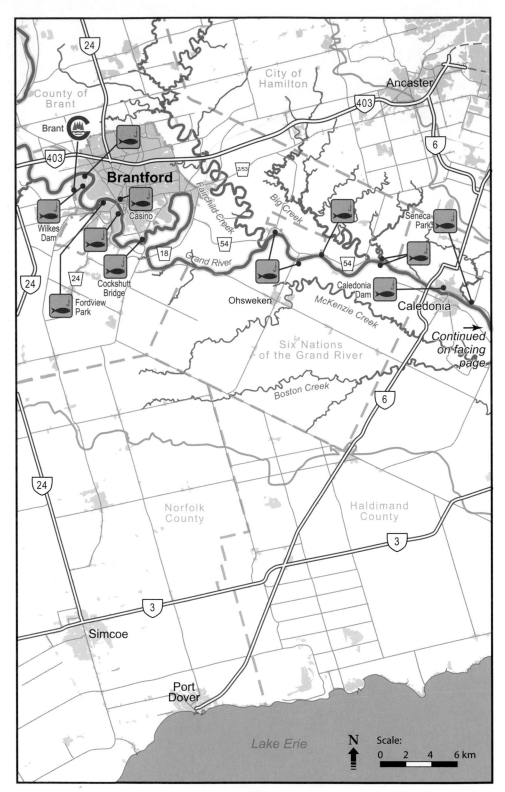

County of Brant

City of Hamilton

Ancaster

403

Brant

24

Brantford

403

Casino

Wilkes Dam

24

Cockshutt Bridge

Fordview Park

Fairchild Creek

Big Creek

2/53

Grand River

54

18

Seneca Park

Caledonia Dam

54

Caledonia

Ohsweken

McKenzie Creek

Continued on facing page

Six Nations of the Grand River

Boston Creek

6

Norfolk County

Haldimand County

3

24

3

Simcoe

Port Dover

Lake Erie

N

Scale:
0   2   4   6 km

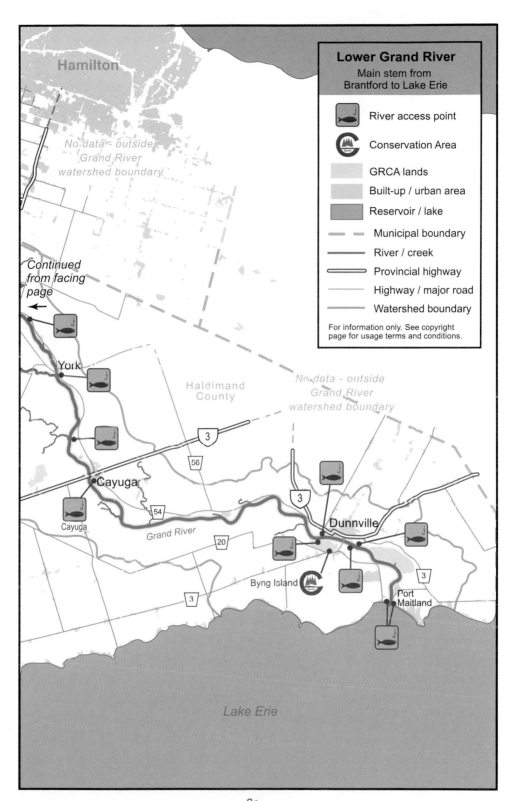

Lower Grand River
Main stem from
Brantford to Lake Erie

River access point

Conservation Area

GRCA lands

Built-up / urban area

Reservoir / lake

Municipal boundary

River / creek

Provincial highway

Highway / major road

Watershed boundary

For information only. See copyright
page for usage terms and conditions.

Hamilton

No data - outside
Grand River
watershed boundary

Continued
from facing
page

York

Haldimand
County

No data - outside
Grand River
watershed boundary

3

56

Cayuga

3

54

Cayuga

Dunnville

20

Grand River

Byng Island

3

Port
Maitland

3

Lake Erie

There is a wheelchair fishing platform just upstream of the Caledonia Dam.

FISHING BRANTFORD TO CALEDONIA

A large "oxbow" immediately south of the City of Brantford provides a mixture of slow water, riffles, and pools. Small boats and motors can be used here with care. Watch for boulders, especially when river flows are low. Anglers who work deeper pools for walleye and smallmouth are often rewarded with good catches. Jigs and smaller crankbaits are popular lures. A spinner with a worm trailer is also a solid bet to get hooked up with these fish. Anglers who fish a medium-sized minnow near bottom can also be quite successful. Don't be afraid to try brightly coloured lures in this stretch of water. Brighter baits seem to be able to draw fish from a greater distance, especially walleye.

Big Creek meets the Grand River between Middleport and Caledonia. Here, big crappies and walleye provide good year-round fishing if you are patient and willing to try a few different spots to find their schools.

This area is especially productive in the early spring and fall for crappie. Anglers who target the flooded bushes and other pieces of cover with small jigs and minnows suspended under a float can be rewarded with good

Caledonia is a hotspot for walleye anglers.

catches. If you don't have luck in these spots, try trolling around with small baits to locate a school of these tasty fish. Crappie generally travel together, and when you find one, there should be more in the area.

Walleye and smallmouth bass are also found in the river above the Caledonia dam all the way up to Brantford. Trolling is a popular technique for walleye. Many anglers also target deeper pool areas with live-bait rigs to find Grand River walleye. Working shoreline cover and mid-river sandbars with jigs, crankbaits, and topwater lures is a popular way of hooking up with the area's smallmouth.

SIGHTS TO SEE: The Pauline Johnson Homestead is a few minutes' drive south at Ohsweken. The Big Creek Boat Farm near Caledonia provides dinner tours on the Grand River.

FOR MORE INFORMATION: Contact Six Nations Tourism at 866-393-3001 or www.sntourism.com.

Grand River Country 866-900-4722 or www.grandrivercountry.com

Archaeology Helps with the Grand's Fishy Past

Paul General, of Six Nations Ecocentre, is a keen amateur archaeologist. Paul has uncovered interesting information about the historical fish community during several archaeological digs that he has done throughout the Grand River watershed.

The artifacts found in archaeological digs provide snapshots of river aquatic life, of wildlife, and of water quality through time. Paul found that the fish species in the digs are different from the species found today. Whitefish, blue pickerel, and various sucker species were the most common species uncovered. Bass, pike, perch, sturgeon, burbot, mooneye, and musky were also regular finds. Some of these fish, such as whitefish, may have been used as trade items, while others were probably taken from the river close to where they were found.

Today in the Grand River, many of the species commonly found in the past are no longer present, or are increasingly rare. The blue pickerel is extinct, and other species, such as muskellunge, whitefish, and sturgeon are no longer present because of water-quality changes or barriers found in the river's lower reaches.

Sturgeon is commonly found in archaeological digs, and it was found as far upstream as Brantford in the 1960s. Nevertheless, it no longer exists in the river because it requires good-quality water and has difficulty navigating obstructions such as dams. If sturgeon could be restored it would be a significant indicator of a healthy watershed. The return of the species will require significant improvements in water quality and fish habitat, and the removal or modification of migration barriers.

CALEDONIA TO DUNNVILLE

SPECIES: Walleye, rainbow trout, smallmouth bass, carp, channel catfish, bullhead, mooneye, black crappie, largemouth bass, northern pike, freshwater drum, redhorse suckers, longnose gar, panfish

Species	Jan	Feb	Mar	Apr	May	June	July	Aug	Sept	Oct	Nov	Dec
Walleye	•	*	*		*	•	•	•	•	*	*	•
Rainbow Trout				•	•				•	*	*	*
Smallmouth bass						•	*	*	*	•		
Catfish				•	*	*	•	•	•	•	•	
Mooneye					•	*	*	•	•			
Crappie			*	*	•	•	•	•	•	•	*	*
Carp				•	•	•	•	•	•			
Suckers				*	*	*						
Gar					*	*	*	*				

FISHING HIGHLIGHTS: From Caledonia to Cayuga, the river is wide and shallow, with small islands, riffles, and holes. These are great spots for canoeists and people wading to find quality angling. The Grand deepens and widens from Cayuga to Dunnville, and is more suited to anglers with power boats.

PUBLIC ACCESS: Access is from road bridges and at community parks on Highway #54, in Caledonia, York, Cayuga, and Dunn-ville. From Cayuga to Dunnville the river is suitable for

Steelhead fall fishing immediately below Caledonia Dam.

powerboating. Public docks are located at Cayuga and Dunnville, along with several private marinas. In addition, a wheelchair-accessible fishing platform is available upstream of the Caledonia Dam.

REGULATIONS: All provincial fishing regulations apply. Fishing is prohibited within 22.9 m (75 ft) downstream of the lower entrance to a fishway.

FISHING CALEDONIA TO DUNNVILLE

Walleye season runs from January 1 to mid-March, before the start of the spawning run. In this part of the river, you will find both migratory and resident walleye. Fish the holes and deep runs with twistertails, minnows, grubs, minnow baits, or even a big dew worm, hopping and dragging it along the bottom. Crappies also provide good fishing through all the seasons, and respond well to small floats, minnows, and tube jigs. Big pike are sometimes caught here, although it is not a prime pike area. In this highly diverse fishery, anglers may find rainbow trout or even the occasional salmon on their lines.

Rainbow trout should be fished only after trout season opens in late April. If you find tagged fish (usually walleye) in this stretch of the Grand

A mixed bag of fish from the Caledonia area.

River, follow the instructions given on the tag for reporting the catch.

From the end of May to mid-June, the big channel catfish move upriver from Lake Erie to spawn. Channel cats are a good size, ranging from a usual 1.5 to 2 kg (3 to 5 lb) to large fish at 9 to 11 kg (20 to 25 lb). Use a float and a worm, or bottom bounce with just a splitshot and a worm. Dunnville celebrates its catfish with a Mudcat Festival on the second weekend in June.

Mooneye also move upriver to spawn in mid-June, providing good fly fishing with a light rod, a floating line, and small flies. These aggressive fish eagerly take dry flies. They can also be targeted with a well-presented nymph. Expect the fish to average 25 to 30 cm (10 to 12 in) with the occasional 33-to-38-cm (13-to-15-in) fish that will really put a bend in a light rod. These fish provide a great opportunity to get new people excited about fly fishing. They are accessible and, during a warm summer evening, there will be lots of fish to get a new angler keen on the sport.

Smallmouth fishing is great in summer, using grubs, tubes, crankbaits,

Galen Yerex with a longnose gar.

topwater baits, woolly buggers, and crayfish patterns in the deeper holes. At this time of the year, bass often forage expansive flats, looking for crayfish, leeches and minnows. Quickly working over mid-depth flats with gravel or cobble bottoms can produce some nice fish. A small popper, fished either on ultralight spinning gear or a fly rod is a great bait to catch numbers of bass and the occasional big boy. The excitement of topwater fishing is addictive, and this portion of the river will help feed this addiction for topwater smallmouth anglers. Make sure you throw your bait near any break in the current — bankside bush, log, or erratic boulder — when covering water. It is surprising how large a bass can come from shallow cover during the summer.

As the water cools in the fall, smallmouth respond well to tubes and grubs as they try to put on weight before the winter. Target deeper holes, where these fish are usually found. This is also a good time to try for crappies. These fish tend to school up and move into their more predictable spring haunts during the cool days of fall. Small minnow-imitating baits or tiny minnows under a float are often successful setups. As with crappie everywhere, dredging the bottom is not the best strategy. These fish usually attack their prey from below, so suspend your bait above them.

Fall is also when migratory rainbow trout or steelhead make the journey up from Lake Erie. Rainbow trout season in this area has been extended to the end of the year. Look for these silver battlers in deeper water with good current flow through it. These fish respond well to a variety of presentations. Many anglers do very well with a float-fishing system and egg sacs, worms, or flies for bait. Fly anglers use an assortment of nymphs, woolly buggers, or egg patterns under a strike indicator, or traditional wet fly-swing techniques with Spey patterns, rabbit strip leeches, and marabou flies that offer a lot of action. Spin anglers can also get involved with medium-sized spinners, spoons, and jigs. Baits that are silver or white are favourites, but if they don't produce, don't hesitate to throw black, chartreuse, or hot-pink baits.

WATER LEVELS: Average low summer flow for this stretch of the Grand River is 19 cms (318 cfs). For current river conditions, call the River Information Line at 519-621-2763 or www.grandriver.ca.

If you fish near Caledonia or Dunnville dams, stay clear of the "boil," or deadly undertow, below the dam. A fishway at the Dunnville Dam enables non-jumping fish, such as walleye, to reach habitat upstream of the dam. Adjustments to the existing fishway are planned for the Caledonia Dam.

SIGHTS TO SEE: The Big Creek Boat Farm hosts dinner and specialty cruises on the Grand River just north of Caledonia. The municipal park adjacent to the Caledonia Dam provides riverside picnic areas, a municipal pool, and a recreation area. Lafortune Park, just north of Caledonia, is a day-use recreation area. Bed-and-breakfast accommodations and a variety of restaurants and gift shops can be found in the area. Caledonia Bait and Tackle near the dam is a great place to pick up gear and current information about the river in this area (www.caledoniabaitandtackle.com).

FOR MORE INFORMATION: Tourism Haldimand 800-863-9607 or www.tourismhaldimand.com

Grand River Country 866-900-4722 or www.grandrivercountry.com

Byng Island Conservation Area

SPECIES: Walleye, rainbow trout, smallmouth bass, northern pike, channel catfish, mooneye, yellow perch, white bass, freshwater drum, crappie, panfish, bullhead, carp

Species	Jan	Feb	Mar	Apr	May	June	July	Aug	Sept	Oct	Nov	Dec
Walleye	*	*			*	•	•	•	•	*	*	*
Rainbow Trout				*	•				•	*	*	*
Catfish				•	*	*	*	•	•			
Pike					*	•	•	•	•	•		
Bass						•	*	*	•	•		
Carp					•	•	•	•	•			
Crappie			*	*	•	•	•	•	•	*	*	

FISHING HIGHLIGHTS: Byng Island Conservation Area in Dunnville provides good family fishing sites from shore and ready access to the Grand River and nearby Lake Erie via the boat launches found in the park.

PUBLIC ACCESS: The GRCA owns 190 ha (470 ac) of land on the west side of the Grand River, with river access and three concrete boat launches. The West End Boat Rental launch provides river access above the Dunnville Dam. The Sulphur Creek launch provides access below the dam and a ten-to-fifteen-minute trip to Lake Erie. There is good family fishing below Weir #4. The conservation area is open from late April until mid-October, and user fees apply. The Dunnville bridge is the last road crossing of the Grand River. Motorists driving to Port Maitland should

Byng Island offers many areas to wet a line.

ensure that they are on the correct side of the Grand for their destination!

FISHING AT BYNG ISLAND CONSERVATION AREA

Byng Island is a favourite spot for many anglers targeting walleye and crappie in the springtime. Fishing around various pieces of cover in the spring can produce good catches of crappie. Walleye anglers target areas of deeper water and also have good success with this popular game fish.

Although the water in this section of the Grand is quite turbid, because of the clay soils of the area, the water quality is fairly good. Noisy fish baits are preferred for this section, because of the silty conditions. The marshes also provide fish habitat, as well as moderating high flows and potential flooding in the river.

In late April and through the fall, rainbow trout are quite common in the waters of Byng Island Conservation Area. As mentioned, noisy lures are the best bet to get hooked up with these acrobatic fish, but egg sacs presented under a float also account for a good number of steelhead. Fishing below the dam is often successful, as fish slow down to get ready to jump over the dam, and this hesitation increases the number of fish to which you can present your bait.

May through June is prime time for channel catfish. These are tenacious battlers and are easily caught with a stinkbait or good old dew worm fished on the bottom. Some anglers also do exceptionally well with spinners baited with a worm. Look for cats both above and below the Dunnville Dam. The catfish in this area can be quite large, so tackle up accordingly to battle fish weighing over 4.5 kg (10 lb).

In the summer, expect to encounter walleye, smallmouth bass, pike, and mooneye in the Byng Island area. Small lures are the way to go for mooneye, and noisy baits will catch you pike and smallmouth bass in the area.

WATER LEVELS: Average summer low flows in this stretch of the river are 19 cms (318 cfs). If you fish near the Dunnville Dam, stay clear of the "boil," or deadly undertow, below the dam. For current river conditions call the River Information Line at 519-621-2763.

SIGHTS TO SEE: Byng Island Conservation Area has 450 serviced and unserviced campsites, computerized reservations, a 0.8-ha (2.0-ac) swimming pool, picnic areas and shelters, showers, four playgrounds, sand volleyball courts, a baseball diamond, a snack bar, canoe and paddleboat rentals, walking trails, and a Visitor Services Program. It is a ten-minute drive to beaches on Lake Erie, and forty-five minutes to Niagara Falls. Local attractions include the Dunnville Mudcat Festival in June, a Bass Derby, and a Walleye Challenge. Scenic attractions include a fifteen-minute drive to Rock Point Provincial Park and Lake Erie beaches. Byng Island is close to the Grand River marshes, the largest freshwater marsh left on the Lake Erie shoreline. Canoeists will enjoy exploring the inlets along the river below the dam.

FOR MORE INFORMATION: Byng Island Conservation Area, 905-774-5755. Internet: www.grandriver.ca

DUNNVILLE TO LAKE ERIE

SPECIES: Walleye, rainbow trout, smallmouth bass, northern pike, channel catfish, mooneye, yellow perch, white bass, white perch, American shad, freshwater drum, crappie, panfish, bullhead, carp, Pacific salmon

Species	Jan	Feb	Mar	Apr	May	June	July	Aug	Sept	Oct	Nov	Dec
Walleye	*	*			*	•	•	•	*	*	*	*
Rainbow Trout				*	•				•	*	*	*
Pike	•	•			*	*	•	•	•			
Bass						•	*	*	*	•	•	
White Bass												
Catfish												
Mooneye												
Crappie												
Bullhead												
Carp				•	•	•	•	•	•			

FISHING HIGHLIGHTS: Although this area offers some of the best walleye fishing spots in southern Ontario, it is the enormous diversity in fish species that attracts anglers. Good fishing can be found in all seasons and for all abilities. This area of the Grand River is a migration route for fish that use both the river and nearby Lake Erie. The dam and fishways in Dunnville are structures that concentrate fish. Migrating walleye,

Fishing on the pier by the lighthouse at Port Maitland.

rainbow trout, suckers, mooneye, American shad, freshwater drum, smallmouth bass, and many more species can be caught in this area, especially through the spring and fall periods. Fishing with lures that create vibrations underwater and with natural baits is most effective in the often heavily stained waters of the Grand's lower reaches.

PUBLIC ACCESS: There are boat launches at Byng Island or from private marinas in Dunnville below the dam. A public boat launch at Port Maitland includes a concrete ramp, parking, picnic area, and washrooms. Shoreline and pier fishing is easily accessible from the parking area. Highway #54 runs along the Grand River from Caledonia to Dunnville. Port Maitland is best accessed from the west side of the Grand River. Cross the Dunnville Bridge and drive south.

Walleye are often easier to catch at dusk or in the dark.

Walleye use both Lake Erie and the Grand for parts of their life cycle.

FISHING THE GRAND RIVER FROM DUNNVILLE TO PORT MAITLAND (LAKE ERIE)

Diversity is the key word for this area. Walleye enthusiasts will be in their element, but surprise catches may include rainbow trout, smallmouth bass, channel catfish, and sheephead. Salmon, sturgeon, and muskellunge catches have also been reported at the mouth of the Grand River. If you find tagged fish, follow the instructions given on the tag for reporting the catch. The GRCA or the Ministry of Natural Resources would also like to hear from you about any unusual catches.

In the spring, walleye congregate in the lower reaches of the Grand River. The Grand is a prime spawning location, and fish from this run contribute significantly to the walleye populations of the eastern basin of Lake Erie. Walleye are encountered by anglers on their way upstream to spawn and, after spawning, on their way back to the lake. Fishing for large fish can be excellent throughout the springtime and again in the fall, as many walleye stage in this area in anticipation of the spring run.

A wide assortment of popular walleye baits and techniques are successful in this area. Trolling the shallow, wide, river flat with crankbaits and bait rigs is popular. Jigs and live bait rigs are also popular with shore-fishing anglers.

Spring is also an excellent time to fish in this area for the river's abundant panfish. The lower reaches of the Grand have abundant black and white crappie. Crappies can be caught in any season with small floats and tube jigs, but the fishing is especially good in the spring. Small minnows are another popular bait to catch this tasty fish. Sunfish are a favourite with young anglers in the southern Grand, and bullheads can make for a good fish fry when caught in the early spring. A big worm fished on the bottom near or after dark is the best way to get hooked up with numbers of bullhead. Top areas for bullheads are in 1 to 1.2 m (3 to 4 ft) of water near expansive cattail areas.

Rainbow trout can be fished after trout season opens in late April. A new, longer season running to the end of December opens new rainbow trout opportunities from Wilkes Dam in Brantford to the mouth of the Grand River. In early summer, rainbow trout respond well to brightly coloured flies, spinnerbaits, worms, and roe. Walleye, pike, bass, mooneye, and channel catfish also provide good summer fishing.

In this highly diverse fishery, anglers may find the occasional salmon on their lines. Species like buffalo, American shad, carp, and freshwater drum can be found.

WATER LEVELS: Average summer low flows in this stretch of the river are 19 cms (318 cfs). For current river conditions call the River Information Line at 519-621-2763 or www.grandriver.ca.

SIGHTS TO SEE: Scenic tours of the Dunnville marshes can be arranged locally. Charter fishing is also available for Lake Erie. Local accommodations include motels, bed-and-breakfast facilities, and camping at Byng Island Conservation Area. Rock Point Provincial Park on Lake Erie, across from Port Maitland, on the east side of the Grand River, also provides camping and day-use facilities. Other attractions include sand beaches at Port Maitland.

FOR MORE INFORMATION: Tourism Haldimand 800-863-9607 or website www.tourismhaldimand.com

Grand River Country 866-900-4722 or www.grandrivercountry.com

WALLEYE WATCHERS

Even though there is an annual catfish festival in Dunnville, the walleye is number one in most anglers' books. There are also a core of dedicated volunteers working with agency staff to ensure that this popular fishery flourishes in the years to come.

A group of volunteers from several clubs, including the Dunnville District Hunters and Anglers, the Port Colborne Conservation Club, and the Fort Erie Conservation Club are all working to improve the Grand River walleye fishery. Volunteers from these clubs and others have been working on a variety of projects in the area for several years. Better walleye fishing is the result.

These clubs have worked in partnership on a variety of activities, all of which have had a positive effect on the local and Lake Erie walleye populations. Projects that have been spearheaded included significant improvements to the spawning ground below the Dunnville Dam and the creation and operation of the Bell Jar hatchery, which sees thousands of walleye produced each year and stocked into the Grand and Welland rivers. These volunteers have also hand-balmed several hundred walleye over the Dunnville Dam to allow them to reach the quality spawning and nursery habitats found between Dunnville and Caledonia.

These groups have been integral to a research project that was conducted from 1999 to 2005 that studied various aspects of the walleye fishery. Activities such as assisting with electro-fishing, netting fish below the dam, and operating the Dunnville Fishway were all important in helping scientists better understand this unique fishery — one that contributes to the river and Lake Erie fisheries.

Thanks to these volunteers fishing in the areas near the Dunnville Dam, and up through to Caledonia remains strong. The OFAH-based "tri clubs" from Dunnville, Port Colborne, and Fort Erie have put several thousand hours into improving fish population. Anglers enjoying good walleye fishing in the Grand and the Eastern basin of Lake Erie have these dedicated individuals to thank for this fishing opportunity.

To get involved contact the OFAH at www.ofah.org.

TRIBUTARIES OF THE GRAND RIVER

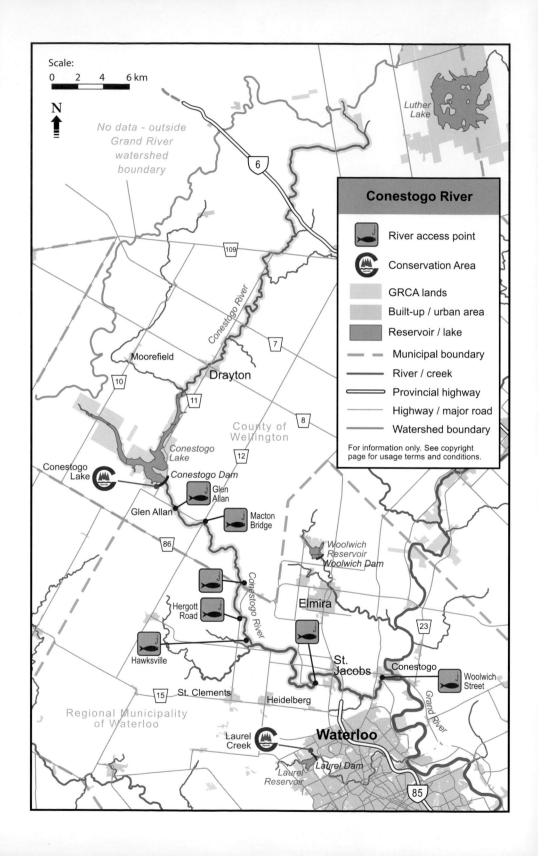

UPPER CONESTOGO RIVER

SPECIES: Northern pike, smallmouth bass, bullhead, carp

Species	Jan	Feb	Mar	Apr	May	June	July	Aug	Sept	Oct	Nov	Dec
Pike					*	*	•	•	*	•		
Bass						*	*	*	*	*	•	
Carp				•	•	•	•	•	•	•		

FISHING HIGHLIGHTS: The Upper Conestogo River is a small river, best accessed by wading. Keep things light and enjoy the peaceful surroundings and relatively small, eager fish.

PUBLIC ACCESS: Drayton, various bridge crossings

FISHING THE UPPER CONESTOGO RIVER

Upstream of Conestogo Lake, the Conestogo River is home to smallmouth bass, northern pike, and carp. The river is small, but the fishing can be good in its deeper runs and pools.

The deep water found in this reach of river provides good spots to find fish of surprising quality, considering the size of the stream. Don't expect monster fish, but using light tackle or a fly rod will make for great sport. For pike, a light metal leader may help reduce the amount of lost tackle. To catch numbers of fish, it is tough to beat a small nymph on a fly rod or a piece of worm under a float with a spinning rod. For lures, choose smaller crankbaits and jigs. Small spinners and topwater baits can also be good options. For pike, medium-weight gear with average bass-sized spinnerbaits and minnow baits are best. Medium- to large-sized minnows fished in the deep, dark depths of a pool can also be effective for both larger bass and pike. The best way to get at these fish is by wading the river. If the water is warm, as it usually is during bass season, this is a pleasant and

Ken Ingram Smith with a nice Conestogo River brown trout.

refreshing way to spend a few hours fishing.

Fishing near bridges that cross the Conestogo is a good bet, as there are often deeper holes near the abutments. Another option is knocking on the doors of farmers who own property on the river. The Conestogo is largely on private property, so access can take a bit of legwork, but it can be fun to explore an area that is lightly fished.

Due to the soils found in the area, even light rain can sometimes cloud the river, making it difficult to fish. Extended dry periods help clear the water and, with lower flows, the fish usually concentrate in the pools. Checking the GRCA's website (www.grandriver.ca) for flows and rainfall in the area is usually a good idea before heading out. Look for relatively dry times with moderate flows at the Drayton flow station.

SIGHTS TO SEE: This is Mennonite country. Enjoy a drive by the well-kept farms and the horses and buggies that travel the roads. Don't be afraid to buy some fresh vegetables, summer sausage, maple syrup, or furniture at farms. But, remember Sunday is not a day to visit these vendors.

FOR MORE INFORMATION: Wellington North Tourism 866-848-3620 or at www.wellington-north.com

CONESTOGO BROWN TROUT FISHERY

A new fishery has recently been created in the tailwater of the Conestogo Dam. The cold waters released from the middle and lower reaches of the Conestogo Reservoir have created a river environment where nutrient-rich cold water is released. This water makes the river ideal habitat for cold-water species like trout. The MNR, Trout Unlimited, the GRCA, and the FOGR have been working together to create this fishery. Brown trout have been stocked in the area since 2003, and they are doing very well according to surveys that have been conducted over the past few years. A handful of volunteers have also pitched in to make this fishery a quality one. These people have helped negotiate and develop access points and stock fish throughout the river, and are now working to improve the local environment and habitat. This group of volunteers is a project of Friends of the Grand River and is called CREW, which stands for Conestogo River Enhancement Workgroup. With the CREW on the job, the Conestogo River should be an angling destination for years to come.

CONESTOGO LAKE CONSERVATION AREA

SPECIES: Northern pike, smallmouth bass, walleye, largemouth bass, bullhead, perch, black crappie, carp

Species	Jan	Feb	Mar	Apr	May	June	July	Aug	Sept	Oct	Nov	Dec
Pike	•	•	•		*	*	•	•	*	•	•	
Bass					*	*	*	*	*	*	•	
Walleye	•	•			•	•	•	•	•	•	•	•
Carp				•	•	•	•	•	•	*		
Panfish	•	•	•	•	•	•	•	•	•	*		

FISHING HIGHLIGHTS: Conestogo Lake is home to smallmouth bass, northern pike, perch, carp, walleye, and largemouth bass. It is best fished by boat. A launch area is available in the Conestogo Lake Conservation Area.

PUBLIC ACCESS: Conestogo Lake is a reservoir located on the Conestogo River about 16 km (10 mi) northwest of Elmira and 11 km (7 mi) south of Drayton. Take County Road #86 west from Elmira to Dorking. Turn right in Dorking and follow the "C" signs to the park entrance. The public can access the upper park and the lower park at Conestogo Lake Conservation Area. The GRCA owns 2266 ha (5,600 ac) at Conestogo Lake, which includes the 735-ha (1,816-ac) lake. Fishing is popular on the lake and in the river below the dam. There is easy access to the water and a double-ramp concrete boat-launch. Powerboating is permitted, and boat and canoe rentals are available. The conservation area is open from the last Friday in April until the middle of October. User fees apply.

Dean McFadden with a big Conestogo Lake bass.

FISHING AT CONESTOGO LAKE CONSERVATION AREA

Pike fishing is excellent year round at Conestogo Lake. During the spring, look for them in the flooded willows along the shore or in shallow, warm bays. During summer and fall, check fish points that jut out into deep water and around creek channels. Use spinnerbaits, jerkbaits, and tube jigs. Live bait rigs fished from shore are also very effective.

Smallmouth bass fishing is on the rise in this lake, with fish of the 2.5-kg (5-lb) class found here. Look for them on points that have deep water close by. Creek channels, old road beds, fence lines, and sunken islands are also good spots. Crankbaits, tube jigs, and topwater baits are most effective.

Perch fishing is good fun for all ages at Conestogo. These fish travel in schools and do a lot of moving, so concentrate on areas that offer some shelter, such as points and sunken humps. In the early season, fish near creeks that flow into the lake. The baits to use are small grub jigs, tube jigs, minnows, and worms.

Walleye fishing on the Conestogo is on the increase, as is fishing for two newer arrivals to this reservoir. Both black crappie and largemouth bass are now found in fishable populations that appear to be expanding.

In the fall, Conestogo water levels are drawn down quite low, and the fish are concentrated. Ice fishing in the winter is an option, but anglers must stay outside the winter-pool area near the dam.

LAKE LEVELS: Conestogo Lake is a large flood-control and water-supply reservoir created by the Conestogo Dam, which is operated by the Grand River Conservation Authority. Water levels are highest in the spring when the lake is filled with water from melting snow and spring runoff. Through the summer and fall, water is released to increase downstream low summer flows, and as a result the lake level gradually drops. Late in the fall, water levels are taken down to low winter levels.

RIVER HEALTH: The GRCA is working with farmers to improve water quality by reducing runoff from farms above Conestogo Lake. During heavy rains or snowmelt, soil and silt can wash from farm fields to the river, carrying nutrients from fertilizers and bacteria from farm manure. Phosphorus is a natural nutrient, and excess amounts cause increased growth of aquatic

The bass population at Conestogo Reservoir is healthy, along with the pike and walleye.

vegetation and algae, resulting in poor water quality. Runoff is most visible when spring thaws or heavy rains turn the river brown with silt carried from the land.

SIGHTS TO SEE: Visitor services at Conestogo Lake include 168 serviced and unserviced campsites, computerized campsite reservations, swimming, water skiing, windsurfing, sailing, picnic areas and shelter, a Visitor Services Program, playgrounds, showers, horseshoe pits, a baseball diamond, volleyball courts, and a self-guided 16-km hiking trail. This is the heart of Mennonite country. Nearby attractions include the Drayton Festival Theatre, fine restaurants, Jakobstettel Guest House, factory outlets, and the St. Jacobs and Kitchener farmers' markets. The Stratford Festival Theatre is a thirty-minute drive.

FOR MORE INFORMATION: Conestogo Lake Conservation Area at 519-638-2873 or www.grandriver.ca

CONESTOGO RIVER TAILWATER

SPECIES: Brown trout, northern pike, walleye, smallmouth bass, suckers, carp

Species	Jan	Feb	Mar	Apr	May	June	July	Aug	Sept	Oct	Nov	Dec
Brown Trout				*	*	*	•	•	*			
Pike					*	*	•	•	•	•		
Bass						•	•	•	•	•		
Carp				•	•	•	•	•	•			

FISHING HIGHLIGHTS: Brown trout have been stocked in the waters below the Conestogo Dam through to past Hawkesville since 2003. This program was initiated by the MNR and the Grand River Fisheries Management Plan partners. It has resulted in this area becoming a destination for trout. The waters of the Conestogo are ideal for this species from the season opener on the fourth Saturday in April through to early July. The cold water released from the bottom-draw dam makes the river a suitable trout habitat downstream to about Hawkesville. A wide variety of fishing techniques are successful here, including the use of various fly patterns, small spinners, plugs, and live baits. In addition to brown trout, northern pike, smallmouth bass, carp, and walleye can also be encountered in the Conestogo tailwater. The water is easily waded in most areas, but a canoe float down the river can open up some excellent opportunities where the water is very lightly fished.

Big brown trout call the Grand River and Conestogo River tailwaters home.

PUBLIC ACCESS: Anglers can access the trout fishery at the lower part of the Conestogo Lake Conservation Area, at Glen Allan, at Macton Bridge, and at the Highway #86 bridge just outside Wallenstein. Wading Is most common, but floating in a canoe opens up a great deal more good trout water. These access locations have been developed in partnership with local landowners, Friends of the Grand River, MNR (Guelph District), and the GRCA.

FISHING THE CONESTOGO RIVER TAILWATER

When the cool waters released from the bottom of the Conestogo reservoir were stocked with trout it was identified as a "Best Bet" recommendation in the Grand River Fisheries Management Plan, due in part to the success seen on the Grand River tailwater below the Shand Dam. The brown trout stocking program was started in 2003, and in 2006 the Canadian Fly Fishing Championships were held on the Grand and Conestogo River tailwaters. But there is a lot more than fly-fishing opportunities on this river; the

The Conestogo River brown trout program is making some anglers happy.

Conestogo has its own unique character.

The cold water releases from the Conestogo Dam result in a cool-water environment below the dam that extends for several miles. Stocked brown trout thrive in the cool, nutrient-rich waters of the Conestogo River downstream to the village of Hawkesville.

The Conestogo River Tailwater is slightly smaller than the Grand Tailwater. Average flows are about 3 cms (106 cfs) in the summertime. Also, upstream of the reservoir the nutrient-rich, clay-based soils are different from the soils found upstream of Belwood Reservoir. For this reason, the

Conestogo is more productive and not as clear as the Grand. Fish that are stocked in the Conestogo each spring grow quickly.

More "nutrients," usually in the form of algae from the lake upstream, mean that fishing on the river is different than that in the clearer waters of the Grand. The Conestogo River has more plant growth on the bottom, and it flows through rolling farmland rather than a more constricted and forested valley. However, the brown trout, northern pike, smallmouth bass, and carp are all quite happy to call the Conestogo home.

The Conestogo River Tailwater is an evolving fishery. The area has long been known as a quality pike-fishing location, but this has declined somewhat in recent years. Since the conditions of the river were identified as being surprisingly similar to the Grand River Tailwater below the Shand Dam, the Ministry of Natural Resources and other partners from the Grand River Fisheries Management Plan Implementation Committee initiated a brown-trout stocking program to create a new dimension to this fishery.

For trout anglers, there are three main fishing methods. Fly fishing is popular, working lures can be very effective, and fishing with baits such as worms and minnows is always productive.

People fly fishing the Conestogo must factor water conditions and clarity into their presentation selection. If the water is clear and there is insect life evident, then break out the dry flies. The fish find it tough to refuse a well-presented caddis pattern if the conditions are right. If there are no flying insects observable, then nymph fishing can be effective. Look for areas of tumbling water that drops into deeper runs and pools. Patterns such as pheasant-tail nymphs, sow bugs, and caddis larvae are all effective.

If the water is a little off-colour, streamers are usually the way to go. Black patterns that cast a good profile are a good bet, as are flies with bulky heads that displace water, making it easier for fish to find them.

Early in the season, streamers are very effective. They also work well later in the season when aquatic weed growth on the bottom and coloured water make dry flies and nymphs much less successful. A fly box for anglers fishing the Conestogo should include a good selection of caddis dry flies, some basic nymph streamers, and a smattering of mayfly imitations. Hendrickson, mahogany, Cahill, and trico hatches are found in the Conestogo Tailwater areas.

CONESTOGO RIVER TAILWATER HATCH CHART

Insect	Apr 1-30	May 1-15	May 16-31	June 1-15	June 16-30	July 1-15	July 16-30	Aug 1-15	Aug 16-31	Sept 1-15	Sept 16-30
BWO	*	*	*				*	*		*	*
Hendrickson			*	*							
Cahills					*	*	*				
Mahogany					*	*					
Trico							*	*			
Black Caddis					*	*	*	*	*		
Tan Caddis				*	*	*	*	*	*	*	*
Grey/Olive Caddis				*	*					*	*
Midges	*	*				*	*	*	*	*	

This chart identifies when these insects are active and when anglers may wish to use artificial flies to imitate them.

For anglers using lures to tempt trout, it is tough to beat a small spinner, although many anglers are very successful with small plugs and spoons. Using the access points and moving around to cover water seems to have more of an effect on success rates than the actual lure selected. Some anglers do very well fishing small jigs. Light gear is easier to handle and makes the smaller trout more sporting. A light-action spinning rod with a 3-kg (6-lb) test is also adequate for landing the larger trout, but if you tie into one of the Conestogo's pike, there is a good chance you will end up short a lure.

Anglers fishing bait can still work deeper pools of the Conestogo Tailwater for a mixed bag of fish. Anglers using worms can expect to catch trout, walleye, carp, suckers, and bass. Those using minnows can expect pike, walleye, trout, and bass. Anglers skilled with float-fishing can target

Tagged walleye.

trout with worms, egg sacs, and small jigs or flies beneath a float. Bass have a soft spot for leeches, and large minnows are usually the way to go to tempt pike or walleye.

Anglers will find pike, bass, and walleye all the way from the dam to past Hawkesville. In this section also look in pools near the end of riffles. Smallmouth bass can be found in rock eddies and deeper pools into which fast water flows. Baits to use are worms, minnows, spinners, jigs, and small shallow-running crankbaits that imitate crayfish or insects. Don't forget to try some topwater baits to experience explosive strikes.

Pike are the most popular species with many longtime Conestogo River anglers. Good catches are frequent in the spring, but catch-and-release is highly recommended to sustain excellent fishing in the future. Pike are common in the large pool at the dam, but some show up in deep pools farther down the river. Baits to use are dead minnow rigs or live minnows, silver spoons, and minnow-imitating baits.

WATER LEVELS: Water levels in the Conestogo River below the dam can rise quickly after heavy rainfall. A warning siren is sounded if significant

James Ingram Smith enjoys the Conestogo brown-trout fishery.

changes in water discharges are going to be made from the dam, and anglers should immediately vacate the area. Normal low summer water levels in the Conestogo River below the dam to the Grand River are 3.5 cms (123 cfs). Current river levels can be obtained from the River Information Line at 519-621-2763 or online at www.grandriver.ca. Fishing is strong from 3.5 cms (123 cfs) through 6 cms (212 cfs). Above these levels, it is more challenging. Above 10 cms (353 cfs), safety is an issue in most areas of the Conestogo, and it is recommended that you look for a different fishing area. You can find up-to-date flow rates at www.grandriver.ca.

SIGHTS TO SEE: This is Mennonite country, and the local farms and their horses and buggies travelling down the road interest many visitors. Take some time to buy some produce or maple syrup from a local farmer. Some farms also sell custom furniture and beautiful quilts. The communities of Hawkesville and Wallenstein have a strong Mennonite influence and are worth exploring.

LOWER CONESTOGO RIVER: HAWKESVILLE TO CONESTOGO

SPECIES: Northern pike, smallmouth bass, carp, redhorse suckers, panfish, walleye

Species	Jan	Feb	Mar	Apr	May	June	July	Aug	Sept	Oct	Nov	Dec
Pike					*	*	•	•	•	*		
Walleye					*	*	•	•	•	*		
Bass						•	*	*	*	•		
Carp				•	•	•	•	•	•	•		

FISHING HIGHLIGHTS: This reach of river has a diverse assortment of warm water fish and the occasional brown trout. There are good access points for wading anglers, but to get at other good fishing areas, a canoe trip is recommended. Anglers targeting pike and bass will find larger concentrations of fish near St. Jacobs and lower down in the Conestogo River system.

PUBLIC ACCESS: You will find access points at the Three Bridges area near St. Jacobs, at Road Crossings at Wallenstein, Hergott Road, Line #85, and Woolwich Street, Conestogo.

FISHING THE LOWER CONESTOGO

The Conestogo River from Hawkesville through to the confluence of the Grand and Conestogo rivers near the village of Conestogo on the outskirts of Waterloo is a fishery that holds a huge variety of warm-water species. Here anglers find pike, walleye, carp, and smallmouth bass. Some of the

The Conestogo River flows though pastoral agricultural countryside.

best smallmouth holes in the entire Grand River watershed are located in the last few miles of the Conestogo River.

Smallmouth bass are most common in waters with slow current and scattered boulders. They can also be found in deeper pools, especially where the river current drops into deeper water. The full range of smallmouth bass baits are effective on the Conestogo, but keep them on the smaller side for more action. Crankbaits, spinners, soft plastic baits, jigs, and topwater baits are all good options. Live bait can be productive, and fly fishers will do well with streamers, woolly buggers, small poppers, grasshoppers, and large nymph imitations.

The river has a good population of all sizes of bass, but, as with any population, there are more small fish. River bass grow slowly, so large fish can be quite old. Studies from rivers similar to the Conestogo have found that smallmouth bass that are 38 cm (15 in) in length can be as much as twenty years old. Larger fish can be even older. For this reason, when you are fishing any river bass population, it is better that you "limit your harvest" rather than "harvest your limit."

Pike fishing on the lower reaches of the Conestogo can be good, especially early in the spring. Target backwater areas and deep, slow pools. Backwater areas are often where the pike have spawned, and the fish usually stay nearby, feeding in the deep water until they get their energy back from the spawn. Lures that imitate a big minnow can be effective, but live- or dead-bait presentations with big minnows on the bottom are tough for a hungry pike to resist. Good catches are frequent in the spring, but catch-and-release is highly recommended to sustain this fishery. Later in the season, pike are more difficult to find, but they are still out there looking for minnow-type baits. In the summer, covering water with spinner baits or large minnow baits, presented in good holding water near concentrations of minnows, is an effective strategy.

SIGHTS TO SEE: The Conestogo flows through the village of St. Jacobs. This town is a very popular destination for tourists and shoppers. It is heavily influenced by its German and Mennonite heritage, and has a wide assortment of shops, boutiques, local markets, and restaurants. There is a nice trail by the millrace in town, and an outlet mall and farmers' market nearby are also popular with visitors.

FOR MORE INFORMATION: St. Jacobs Country at 1-800-265-3353 or www.stjacobs.com

Woolwich Township tourism 519-669-6000 or www.woolwich.ca

Grand River Country 866-900-4722 or www.grandrivercountry.com

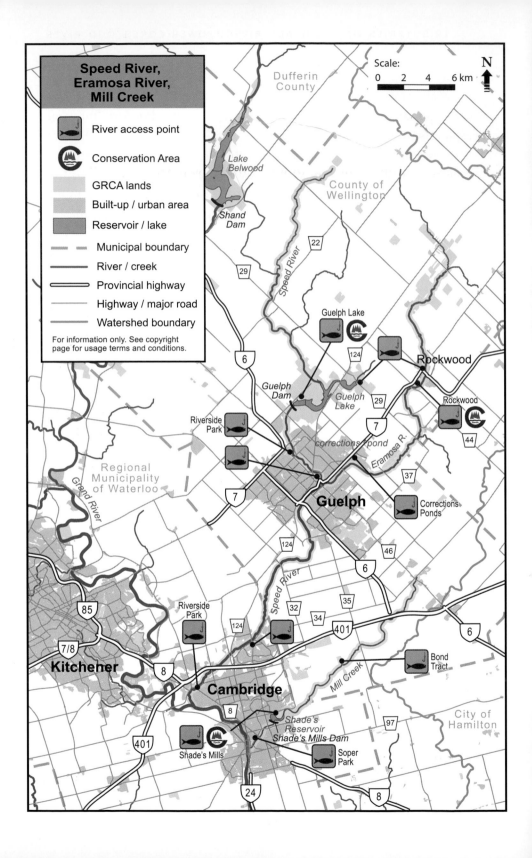

UPPER SPEED RIVER: ABOVE GUELPH LAKE

SPECIES: Brook trout, rainbow trout, brown trout, smallmouth bass, white sucker.

Species	Jan	Feb	Mar	Apr	May	June	July	Aug	Sept	Oct	Nov	Dec
Brown Trout				*	*	*	•	•	*			
Brook Trout				*	*	*	•	•	*			

FISHING HIGHLIGHTS: This is the most heavily forested portion of headwater stream in the entire watershed, and the upper Speed River is home to naturally reproducing trout populations.

PUBLIC ACCESS: Most of the upper Speed River runs through private property. Seeking landowner permission to gain access to this water is required.

FISHING THE UPPER SPEED RIVER

The Speed River flows through a largely forested watershed, and the water quality and temperature in much of the upper Speed River provide good trout habitat. The river is relatively small through most of this area, and its forested nature makes it a challenge to fish in many spots, but fly fishers using a short, light rod can have fun with the abundant trout. Having a good generic set of flies that includes dry flies, nymphs, and streamers, should be adequate in most locations on the Speed. There is healthy aquatic life on this river, so be ready for typical southern-Ontario hatches of mayflies and caddis flies.

Flies that anglers will want to have on hand include elk-hair caddis flies in sizes #18 to #14 in tan and olive, mayfly imitations such as the Adams,

The well-forested upper Speed River holds good quality trout fishing.

white Wulff, and various parachute patterns in sizes #12 to #20. A stimulator or other stonefly pattern and a grasshopper pattern or two should cover your dry-fly needs. For use under the surface, you should be ready with basic nymphs, such as the gold-ribbed hare's ear, red squirrel nymph, black stonefly, and prince nymph. Include a handful of streamers, such as realistic patterns to imitate sculpins and brighter attractor patterns. Patterns such as muddler minnows, woolly buggers, spruce flies, and grey ghosts can all be effective.

Anglers using spinning tackle should use ultralight tackle to best present small baits to the fish in tight quarters. Small spinners and live bait are good bets for this type of trout fishing. A #0 or #1 spinner with a piece of worm attached is tough to beat for probing under log-jams and into deep holes.

GUELPH LAKE CONSERVATION AREA

SPECIES: Smallmouth bass, largemouth bass, black crappie, northern pike, yellow perch, bullhead, carp

Species	Jan	Feb	Mar	Apr	May	June	July	Aug	Sept	Oct	Nov	Dec
Bass					*	*	*	*	*	•		
Pike	•	•			*	*	•	•	•	*	*	
Crappie	•	•		*	*	•	•	•	•	•		
Perch	*	*		*	•	•	•	•	•	•		

FISHING HIGHLIGHTS: This reservoir has very healthy populations of many warm-water species. During open water season, it is best fished from a non-motorized boat, but there are some shoreline fishing areas that are productive. In the winter, anglers try for perch and pike through the ice.

PUBLIC ACCESS: Guelph Lake Conservation Area is located on the Speed River on the northeast edge of the City of Guelph. Travelling north on Highway #6 out of Guelph, turn right onto Guelph Township Road #6 and follow the signs. The GRCA owns 1608 ha (3,971 ac) of land and water at Guelph Lake, with easy shore access and several crude gravel boat ramps. The park is open from the last Friday in April until the middle of October and admission fees apply. The conservation area also has a gravel boat launch. *Note that gasoline engines are not allowed on this reservoir.

Guelph Dam.

FISHING AT GUELPH LAKE CONSERVATION AREA

Guelph Lake is a large flood-control and water-supply reservoir created by the Guelph Dam, which is operated by the Grand River Conservation Authority. The reservoir, built in 1976, covers stump fields, former roads, and building foundations, which provide excellent cover for fish. Willows and other shoreline vegetation also support good fish populations. As with other GRCA reservoirs, water levels are highest in the spring when the lake is filled with water from melting snow and spring runoff. Through the summer and fall, lake levels drop gradually as water is released to add to otherwise low summer flows. In late fall, lake levels are drawn down to winter levels, which are low.

Pike fishing at Guelph Lake is at its prime in the early spring, when the big fish move into the flooded willows and the shallow, weedy areas at the edge of the lake. At this time, use big, brightly coloured spinnerbaits, spoons, minnow baits, and jerkbaits. Summer pike fishing is somewhat slower, although still a good option with crankbaits and spinnerbaits. In the fall, as water levels drop, some big fish can be caught on jigs fished at deeper water structures, such as river channel ledges.

Spring is also a great time to target the reservoir's abundant panfish population. Perch and crappie move into shallows to spawn in the spring and can be reached by anglers fishing from shore. Nevertheless, the willows that line the lake are excellent habitat for these fish and here they are better reached from the water side. A small boat or canoe can get anglers in just the right place to take advantage of these fish.

Summer at Guelph Lake is smallmouth bass heaven. Trophy-sized fish over 50 cm (20 in) are caught regularly in the lake's abundant deep-water structures. Look for hotspots such as submerged roadbeds by lining yourself up with old road alignments visible at the lake edge. Use grubs, tubes, crankbaits, and topwater lures in the summer. Later in the season, use tube jigs, jigging spoons, or a grub, and fish vertically over structures such as river channel bends, old fencerows, or humps.

Summer is also the time to find largemouth bass in the back bays. They respond well to a Texas-rigged plastic worm, crayfish spinnerbaits, or good topwater lures like a Zara-spook or a Pop-R.

Crappies provide year-round fishing. Look for them after the ice is out in shallows, back bays, and flooded timber, and in the rip-rap area found along Highway #24. Slip floats, and little crappie tubes or twistertail jigs with little minnows are the lures of choice. In the summer, a fish-finder is useful, as crappies school up and suspend over structures about 2 to 3 m (8 to 10 ft) off the bottom. Nevertheless, once you find the right spot over a school, you can do really well.

REGULATIONS: All provincial fishing regulations apply. Gasoline-powered boats are not allowed on Guelph Lake, although electric motors can be used. Fishing from the dam and adjacent rip-rap walls is prohibited.

SIGHTS TO SEE: Guelph Lake Conservation Area provides 350 serviced and unserviced campsites, computerized reservation of campsites, two swimming beaches, canoe rentals, hiking trails, and picnic areas and

Family fishing at the Guelph Corrections Ponds.

shelters. The lake is popular with windsurfers and home to a local sailing club.

Seasonal events at the park include the Hillside Music Festival in July, provincial-level triathlons, and fishing derbies. Nearby attractions include the Guelph Spring Festival in May, the Jazz Festival in September, a lively Saturday farmers' market, and many other events. A wide variety of accommodations and restaurants suit every vacation budget.

FOR MORE INFORMATION: Guelph Visitor and Convention Services 519-837-1335 or at www.visitguelphwellington.ca

For Guelph Lake Conservation Area, phone 519-824-5061.

Grand River Country 866-900-4722 or www.grandrivercountry.com

CORRECTIONS PONDS, GUELPH

This site is located off of York Road on the east side of Guelph. Parking can be found in the lots for the baseball diamonds in the area. The two ponds contain a wide assortment of warm-water fish. Bass, pike, crappie, rock bass, and sunfish are the most common species encountered here.

AQUATIC SPECIES AT RISK IN THE GRAND WATERSHED

The Grand River is a unique environment, and it is home to some of the rarest fish in Canada. Out of the thirty aquatic species that are of special concern, threatened, or endangered under Committee on the Status of Endangered Wildlife in Canada, nine are from the Grand River Watershed.

A recovery action group is tackling the challenges associated with securing existing populations of species at risk and re-establishing them in parts of their historic range.

These species include the silver shiner, the redside dace, the greenside darter and river redhorse, the black redhorse, and the Eastern sand darter. In addition, two endangered mussel species are found in the Grand, including the wavy-rayed lamp-mussel and the round pigtoe. Other species that have been found include grass pickerel, lake sturgeon, and bigmouth buffalo.

Many of these species are threatened by poor water quality caused by runoff from farmlands, urban development, and erosion. Dams also have an impact on these species by preventing colonization of additional areas, by fragmenting already declining populations, or by bringing about the temperature change caused by impounded water.

There is a recovery team and a Recovery Strategy for Fishes

at Risk in the Grand River. The Grand River Fisheries Management Plan also contains details of actions to address concerns surrounding these species. Surveys are being completed to determine species distributions and important habitat areas.

Thanks to public outreach activities, local residents have a better understanding of the species at risk and the ongoing recovery activities in the watershed.

As we work to improve the environment in the Grand River, we will be able to sustain healthy fish populations that include some of these threatened species.

For more information about Species at Risk in the Grand River contact the Ministry of Natural Resources, Guelph District Office, at 519-826-4955.

LOWER SPEED RIVER: BELOW GUELPH LAKE

SPECIES: Smallmouth bass, largemouth bass, northern pike, bullhead, carp, and panfish

Species	Jan	Feb	Mar	Apr	May	June	July	Aug	Sept	Oct	Nov	Dec
Carp				•	*	*	•	•	•	•	•	
Bass						•	•	•	•	•	•	
Pike					•	•	•	•	•	•	•	
Bullhead				*	•	•						

FISHING HIGHLIGHTS: The Speed River is a warm-water river with good smallmouth bass and black crappie fishing near the Guelph Lake dam and into Guelph. This reach of the river is best fished by wading along the Royal Trail. Further downstream, this warm river improves for pike, carp, and largemouth bass right through into Cambridge, where it enters the Grand. In this area a canoe is often helpful to access fishing areas.

PUBLIC ACCESS: The Speed can be accessed via the Royal Trail, with parking along Victoria Road, Riverside Park in Guelph off Gordon Street, and at the River Run Centre downtown. Farther downstream, road crossings provide access to the river. Riverside Park nearer the mouth of the Grand off Eagle Street in Cambridge is another popular access point.

The Speed below Guelph Reservoir is a cool-water fishery.

Fishing the Lower Speed River

Smallmouth fishing is the prime attraction in the Speed River, and even in the centre of the City of Guelph anglers can expect to find bass. Grubs, tube jigs, and topwater lures are all effective. Keeping baits on the small side will help increase the numbers of fish you will find. In Cambridge (Preston), good smallmouth fishing is found in the stretch of the river from Riverside Park to the confluence with the Grand River. For a change of pace, large carp, 9 kg (20 lb) and over, can be caught in Riverside Park, using corn kernels, dough balls, and worms.

Normal low summer flows in the Speed downstream of the city are 2.5 cms (88.3 cfs). For information on current water levels, call the River Information Line at 519-621-2763 or visit www.grandriver.ca.

New Life for Marden Creek

The brook trout of Marden Creek must feel like Mark Twain's famous character Tom Sawyer while witnessing his funeral. No one had seen a trout in this Guelph area stream for over thirty years. However, the news of their demise has indeed been greatly exaggerated.

Enter the Wellington County Stewardship Council (WCSC). The council "adopted" the creek and began restoration in 2001. Since then, the members have removed dams, narrowed the stream channel, planted trees, and collected temperature and fish-population data. More recently, the Guelph Chapter of Trout Unlimited Canada has joined them in their mission.

In 2005, it was confirmed that a small and fragile population of native trout still persisted in the stream's headwaters. Since 2005, the population of brook trout has responded well to restoration efforts, and is expanding. The partners hope that their work will help these fish repopulate the entire stream, and perhaps eventually result in a seasonal fishery in the Speed River below the Guelph Dam. For more information, contact Wellington County Stewardship Council at 519-826-4936.

Eramosa River

Species: Rainbow trout, brown trout, brook trout

Species	Jan	Feb	Mar	Apr	May	June	July	Aug	Sept	Oct	Nov	Dec
Brook Trout					*	*	•	•	•			
Brown Trout					*	*	•	•	•			
Small-mouth Bass						•	•	•	•	•		
Carp				*	•	•	•	•	•	•		

Fishing the Eramosa River

The Eramosa River flows through a largely forested watershed. The water quality and temperature in much of the upper Eramosa provide good trout habitat; however most of this river flows through private land. Landowner permission is required to get to the river, which may get you access to some excellent and lightly fished trout water. Because this is a small, well-forested river, fly fishers should use a shorter rod and watch their back casts to avoid cedars and willows. In a small river that receives little fishing pressure, top patterns are often generic dry flies, nymphs, and streamers. On the surface, an elk-hair caddis or Adams dry fly in sizes from #18 to #12 can work very well. Attractor patterns like the Royal Coachman, Au Sable Wulff, Despair, and Renegade can also be very productive. Under the surface, a bead-headed gold-ribbed hare's ear is tough to beat, but pheasant-tail nymphs and prince nymphs will also produce. For a change of pace try swinging a wet fly such as a hare's ear, a professor, or a partridge and orange into areas that are difficult to cast to. It would be worth having streamers available, such as a muddler minnow, a Mickey Finn, or a woolly bugger.

Anglers will also do well with small spinners, especially if they have a

The Eramosa River holds quality trout fisheries in its well-forested reaches.

small piece of worm attached to the hook. When flows are slightly elevated after a spring storm, swinging a spinner through a pool that has some cover in it or along it can bring fantastic results. Floating a worm under log-jams and undercut banks can also be very effective. In the summer, try replacing the worm with a freshly caught grasshopper. Dropping a hopper on the water near a grassy undercut bank is a sure way to see some of the Eramosa's trout population up close. As with all small streams, it is best to keep tackle simple and light. A short ultralight spinning rod is ideal to work this river.

Closer to the Rockwood Reservoir, the Eramosa River, which feeds the reservoir, is relatively slow moving. Upstream ponds, beaver dams, and fallen trees slow it down considerably. This is warmer water, suitable for fish like bass and panfish. Rehabilitation has been carried out on several of its tributaries. Blue Springs Creek, a tributary of the Eramosa, is considered to be one of the most pristine creeks in southern Ontario.

Below the Rockwood Reservoir to the confluence with the Speed River in Guelph, the Eramosa River has a warm-water fishery. Anglers can expect to find smallmouth bass, suckers, bullheads, panfish, and carp in this reach of river.

ROCKWOOD CONSERVATION AREA

SPECIES: Smallmouth bass, largemouth bass, carp, rainbow trout, carp, bullhead

Species	Jan	Feb	Mar	Apr	May	June	July	Aug	Sept	Oct	Nov	Dec
Rainbow Trout				*	*	•	•		•			
Bass						•	•	•	•	•		
Carp					•	•	•	•	•			

FISHING HIGHLIGHTS: Rockwood is a scenic area that has something for everyone, including many recreational activities. The spring fishing for stocked rainbow trout is a highlight.

PUBLIC ACCESS: The GRCA owns 79 ha (195 ac) of land with a former mill pond. Access is through the Rockwood Conservation Area and entrance fees apply. Non-motorized boating is permitted. The park is located on the Eramosa River, about 10 km (6 mi) northeast of Guelph. From Highway 401, take Guelph Line exit north and turn right on Highway #7. Watch for Rockwood Conservation Area signs on the right.

FISHING ROCKWOOD CONSERVATION AREA

The reservoir at Rockwood is a scenic and easily accessible place to wet a line. Each spring rainbow trout are stocked in the reservoir. After the trout fishing opener until late May there is good fishing for these fish using a float and bait like a worm or egg sac. Another option is to cast a small spinner or spoon to the fish. Fly fishers can use an assortment of nymphs, dry flies, and streamers in hopes of attracting a cruising rainbow. Good areas to target are the outflow area of the former upper pond by the mill ruins, and along the

Rockwood Conservation area stocks its pond with trout each season.

dam at the lower end of the reservoir. It is common to see trout feeding on the surface from the dam area or the beach every spring. This is a great time to get a family out for a fishing adventure.

As the water warms, the trout fishing slows, but the bass fishing improves. Once the bass season opens near the end of June, the fishing is usually pretty good. Due to the often-turbid nature of Rockwood Reservoir, surface baits that create a good disturbance and baits like spinnerbaits in bright colours are usually the most effective. The reservoir is home to a modest population of generally smallish bass, but every year there are stories of big bass coming from Rockwood. Bass anglers may also hook up with sunfish or carp, especially if they are using live bait such as worms.

SIGHTS TO SEE: Natural features include limestone cliffs and glacial potholes. The Devil's Well near Rockwood Conservation Area is the world's largest pothole formation. History buffs will enjoy the old Harris Mill ruins. Rockwood features more than a hundred campsites and great hiking trails, canoe rentals, and swimming.

FOR MORE INFORMATION: Phone Rockwood Conservation Area at 519-856-9543 or www.grandriver.ca.

MILL CREEK, CAMBRIDGE

SPECIES: Brown trout, brook trout, smallmouth bass

Species	Jan	Feb	Mar	Apr	May	June	July	Aug	Sept	Oct	Nov	Dec
Brown Trout				•	*	*	*	•	*			
Brook Trout				•	*	*	•	•	*			

FISHING HIGHLIGHTS: Mill Creek is a small stream that has a good population of brown trout. Much of it is privately owned, but there are some public fishing sites at the Bond Tract and in downtown Cambridge.

PUBLIC ACCESS: For upper Mill Creek, you gain access from the Bond Tract. From Highway 401, exit at 286, Townline Road, Cambridge, south to the First Line. Turn right on the First Line, and watch for Ministry of Natural Resources Tract signs. Observe fish-sanctuary regulations in this area. Soper Park in downtown Cambridge is a place to access Mill Creek below the Shade's Mills Reservoir.

FISHING IN MILL CREEK

Mill Creek is a healthy cold-water stream impounded by a small dam at the east end of Cambridge. Above the reservoir, the stream is spring fed and runs through mostly forested areas. Rehabilitation efforts have also improved the water quality and fish habitat. Much of this area is privately owned, and seeking landowner permission is required to fish Mill Creek here.

Below Shade's Mills reservoir, the creek becomes urbanized, and at one point disappears into a culvert before reaching the Grand River. Brown trout are stocked in the Soper Park area in downtown Cambridge downstream of

The Mill Creek Stewardship Rangers complete another stream restoration project.

Shade's Mills Reservoir, and are naturally reproducing above the reservoir.

Above the reservoir, the Ministry of Natural Resources has provided access and parking at the Bond Tract. For anglers accustomed to fishing small cedar-lined streams, the area is suitable for fly fishing for brown trout and brook trout, with generic dry fly and nymph patterns or small streamers. But be prepared to lose a few floes to the trees and woody debris found in the creek.

The tight quarters are often easier fished with spinning gear. Spinners representing injured minnows look like an easy meal for hungry browns later in the season. Other popular lures include small minnow baits and crankbaits, as well as small jigs in some of the deeper pools. Fishing with a worm and a small split shot is always a good bet. A small, weighted spinner can drag up fish from under cedar blowdowns and around log-jams in this part of Mill Creek if you get the bait right down into the wood. On a stream of this size, being stealthy is important. Shadows on the water and vibrations from heavy footsteps on the riverbank can really decrease an angler's success rate.

REGULATIONS: All provincial fishing regulations apply. Mill Creek was formerly known as Galt Creek, and is referred to as such in the 1999

Provincial Fishing Regulations. A fish sanctuary is in effect from upstream of the boundary of North Dumfries and Puslinch Townships, including Aberfoyle Creek. No fishing is permitted in this area from October 1 to the Friday before the last Saturday in April.

MILL CREEK STEWARDSHIP
RANGERS: A COMMUNITY PARTNERSHIP IN ACTION

The Mill Creek Stewardship Ranger program is an example of government and business working together to help local youth and the environment. A crew of four youths and a supervisor have been spending the summers since 2002 completing environmental restoration projects on Mill Creek in Puslinch Township.

This unique program is supported by the Ontario Trillium Foundation, the Grand River Conservation Authority, the Ministry of Natural Resources, Puslinch Township, and many local businesses. The program provides the opportunity for youth to learn about their environment in a hands-on way. They really do get their hands dirty and roll rocks in the creek to make a tangible difference.

In past seasons, the crew has built cedar deflectors in the stream to adjust the channel and stabilize stream banks, erected fencing to keep cattle out of the creek, and built rock pods to provide cover for fish. They have completed electro-fishing assessments and repaired roads damaged by excessive ATV use. These students also have an opportunity to work with corporate partners in the gravel and water-bottling business to learn more about using and managing our natural resources.

Most of the students involved with the program have aspirations to work in the environmental field. These are the people who will be directing our future. The Stewardship Ranger program provides an ideal summer job and an environmental learning experience. For more information about this program contact the GRCA at 519-621-2761 in Cambridge.

SHADE'S MILLS CONSERVATION AREA

SPECIES: Smallmouth bass, largemouth bass, northern pike, yellow perch, rock bass, sunfish, bullhead, carp

Species	Jan	Feb	Mar	Apr	May	June	July	Aug	Sept	Oct	Nov	Dec
Bass						•	•	•	*	•		
Pike	*	•	•		*	*	•	•	•	*		
Panfish	*	•	•	•	*	*	•	•	•			
Carp					•	•	•	•	•			

FISHING HIGHLIGHTS: Shade's Mills is a productive warm-water fishery with easy access to panfish, pike, and bass. A non-motorized boat can get you to excellent fish habitat around weed beds, stumps, and rocky shoals. From shore there are excellent places to hook up with panfish. This is a family-friendly location.

PUBLIC ACCESS: The GRCA owns 177 ha (437 ac) of land on Mill Creek and around the reservoir. Access is through the conservation area, and user fees apply. Non-motorized boating is permitted, and canoe rentals are available. The conservation area is open for day use only from the Saturday of the Victoria Day weekend in May until the middle of September, and then again in the winter for ice fishing and cross-country skiing. The conservation area is located at the eastern edge of the City of Cambridge on Mill (Galt) Creek. Follow Franklin Boulevard and watch for the conservation area signs. Turn east at Avenue Road and look for the park gates on your right.

Shade's Mills is a good place to get out and enjoy fishing .

FISHING SHADE'S MILLS RESERVOIR

This reservoir is home to healthy populations of warm-water fish. Early in the spring the season starts with panfishing. Perch, rock bass, and sunfish are abundant in this lake and easy to target for anglers who use small lures or natural baits. This is also a time of year when these fish are quite accessible from shore. They use the shoreline vegetation as cover to spawn and forage.

In mid-May, pike season opens, and these fish can be best targeted by boat. Use spinner baits of minnow-imitating lures in bright, or panfish-mimicking, colours, since the pike will be trying to ambush panfish in the shallows and around emerging weed clumps. The boat-launch area has been improved recently, and fishing boats can now easily be floated on the reservoir. Use of gas-powered motors is prohibited, but a popular alternative is a boat with the gas motor pulled up and an electric motor on the bow.

Once bass season opens, the largemouth and smallmouth bass in this reservoir become fair game. They can be caught with a full assortment of lures designed for this species, but a jig and pig and tube jigs fished in the deep weed edges and around stumps can be very effective. Drop-shotting is also a popular way to finesse bass that are holding near weed lines. To cover more water and search for aggressive fish, pull out a spinnerbait. If the weed growth is not too thick, jerkbaits can be effective. If the weeds are getting

Shade's Mills is located in Cambridge and offers good fishing for panfish, bass, and pike.

thicker, try a soft plastic jerkbait rigged "Texposed" to get at the fish or Texas rig a plastic worm and probe it through cover.

In winter, some anglers fish Shade's Mills in search of perch and northern pike. Minnows are the most popular bait, but many anglers catch good numbers of perch with small spoons and other finesse perch rigs.

WATER LEVELS: The reservoir is drawn down in late fall to accommodate spring snowmelt and rainfall. For current water temperatures in Mill Creek, call the River Information Line at 519-621-2763 or online at www. grandriver.ca.

SIGHTS TO SEE: Nearby attractions include Cambridge's historic buildings and riverside park system, a wide variety of restaurants, and accommodations.

FOR MORE INFORMATION: phone the park at 519-621-3697 or www. grandriver.ca.

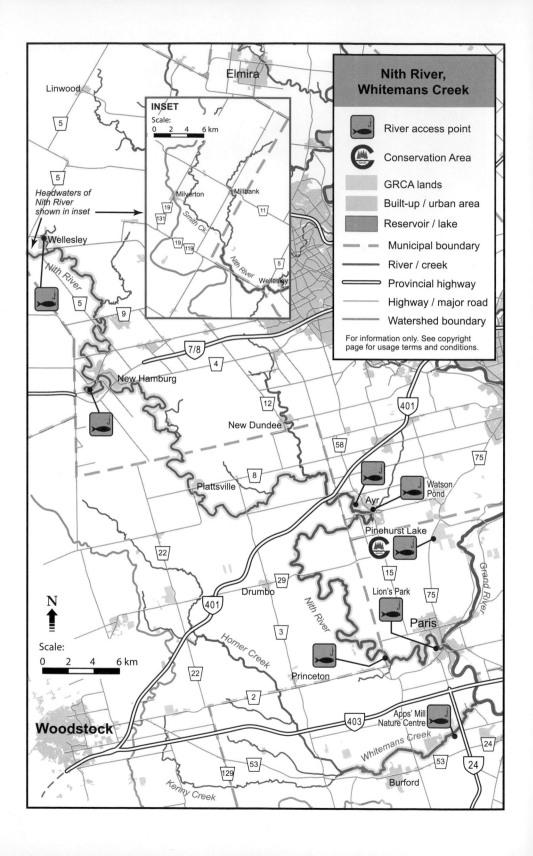

Nith River, Whitemans Creek

River access point

Conservation Area

GRCA lands

Built-up / urban area

Reservoir / lake

Municipal boundary

River / creek

Provincial highway

Highway / major road

Watershed boundary

For information only. See copyright page for usage terms and conditions.

Linwood

Elmira

INSET
Scale:
0 2 4 6 km

Milverton

Millbank

19
131

Smith Ck.

11

19
119

Nith River

5

Wellesley

Headwaters of
Nith River
shown in inset

Wellesley

Nith River

5

5

9

5

7/8

4

New Hamburg

12

New Dundee

401

58

75

Plattsville

8

Ayr

Watson
Pond

22

Pinehurst Lake

29

15

Drumbo

Nith River

Lion's Park

75

401

3

Paris

N

Scale:
0 2 4 6 km

Horner Creek

Grand River

22

Princeton

2

Woodstock

403

Apps' Mill
Nature Centre

Whitemans Creek

24

24

53

129

53

Burford

Kenny Creek

NITH RIVER: NEW HAMBURG, AYR, TO PARIS

SPECIES: Smallmouth bass, walleye, northern pike, rainbow trout, redhorse suckers, carp, panfish

Species	Jan	Feb	Mar	Apr	May	June	July	Aug	Sept	Oct	Nov	Dec
Small-mouth Bass						*	*	*	*	•		
Pike	•	•	*		•	•	•	•	•			
Walleye	•	•	•		•	*	•	•	•	*	•	
Carp				•	•	•	•	•	•			

FISHING HIGHLIGHTS: New Hamburg to Ayr, for walleye in the early spring (March). Ayr to Canning for smallmouth fishing. Ayr to Paris for smallmouth, pike, and rainbow trout.

PUBLIC ACCESS: This section of the Nith River flows southeast from New Hamburg to Paris on the Grand River. New Hamburg can be accessed from Highways #7 and #8, west of Kitchener. Paris can be reached from Highway 403 at the Highway #2 exit. The Nith River is fairly secluded, and is navigable only by canoe below New Hamburg, although frequent shallow spots may be difficult. You can access the water from the many road bridges crossing the Nith and from Lion's Park in Paris.

The Nith River in "downtown" Ayr.

FISHING THE NITH RIVER

Above New Hamburg, the Nith River receives surface drainage from river-side farming operations, resulting in poor water quality, especially during the summer months. Below New Hamburg, water quality improves, and is quite good in the lower reaches near Paris.

From New Hamburg to Ayr, early spring anglers (before March 31) can find 3-to-4-kg (7-to-8 lb) walleye using yellow or white twistertails and small crankbaits. Once trout season opens, dropback rainbows are available until late May, using traditional steelhead methods.

During the summer, from Ayr downriver to Canning, fine smallmouth fishing can be found in the deep pools and behind boulders with grubs and tubes. Smallmouth fishing continues to be excellent right through to Paris. Although pike may be found in this section, the river is predominantly smallmouth habitat.

The Nith River in Paris is a popular park area.

WATER LEVELS: Normal summer low flows for the Nith River at New Hamburg are 1.5 cms (53 cfs), and at Ayr 3 cms (106 cfs). For current levels contact the River Information Line at 519-621-2763 or www.grandriver.ca. **SIGHTS TO SEE:** New Hamburg boasts the largest operating waterwheel in North America. Nearby attractions include Castle Kilbride in Baden.

FOR MORE INFORMATION: Waterloo Region Tourism at 877-585-7517 or www.explorewaterlooregion.com

WATSON POND, AYR

This pond is located in downtown Ayr. Access is easy from either Highway 401 or Highway #24. Off Northumberland Street take Gibson Street to find the parking lot beside the library on the north side of the park. The pond has been stocked with rainbow trout, and there are also smallmouth bass present.

Fishing at Watson Pond, right in downtown Ayr.

Whitemans Creek: From Burford to the Grand River

Species: Brown trout, rainbow trout, brook trout

Species	Jan	Feb	Mar	Apr	May	June	July	Aug	Sept	Oct	Nov	Dec
Rainbow Trout				*	*	*	*	*	*			
Brown Trout				•	*	*	*	*	*			
Brook Trout				•	•	•	•	•	•			

Fishing Highlights: This small river's cool water, riffles, and occasional deep pools make this a prime area for trout. Whitemans is popular with fly and bait anglers, and has a healthy trout population that responds well to a variety of baits. It is a key steelhead nursery stream and its log-jams are home to trophy brown trout. Special regulations affect portions of this stream, and are helping maintain this quality fishery.

Public Access: The GRCA owns 108 ha (266 ac) of land on both sides of Whitemans Creek at Apps' Mill Nature Centre, near Brantford. The creek can be accessed from Robinson Road, Brantford, on GRCA property, and from Lion's Park on Maple Avenue, Burford. Whitemans Creek passes through Burford Township before entering the Grand River about 5 km (3 mi) below Paris. From Highway 403, turn south on Rest Acres Road, and right on Robinson Road to the road bridge over Whitemans Creek.

Whitemans Creek is a quality trout stream and nursery area for a good portion of the Grand River steelhead run.

REGULATIONS: Special regulations are posted between Robinson Road and Cleaver Sideroad. Catch and possession limits must be observed, and artificial lures with a barbless hook must be used. Anglers are allowed to harvest one trout over 50 cm (20 in) per day. Whitemans Creek from the East Quarter Townline Road to the Grand River is a designated fish sanctuary, with no fishing from October 1 to the Friday before the last Saturday in April. All other provincial fishing regulations apply.

FISHING WHITEMANS CREEK

Whitemans Creek is a fast-flowing, cold-water tributary that has responded well to community, GRCA, and MNR rehabilitation efforts over the past few years. Special angling regulations are in place to encourage the growth of a sustainable fishery. This small river is very popular with fly-fishing anglers.

The fishing can be good throughout the season. Near opening day, the Hendrickson hatch is one that attracts many anglers. This is the first good dry-fly fishing of the season. As the water warms a bit into the spring, other hatches follow. Anglers should be prepared with March browns, sulphurs, Cahills, lead-wing coachmen, and small mahoganies. This stream is also home to a good population of caddis files. Seasoned Whitemans anglers have a good assortment of medium-sized caddis imitations in tan and olive-grey. In order to fish Whitemans, you should have a good assortment of elk-hair caddis, Adams, white Wulffs, and other match-the-hatch patterns for fishing on the surface during a hatch.

For fishing below the surface, anglers should have a good assortment of mayfly nymphs, caddis larvae, and caddis pupae imitations. Flies like Lafontaine's sparkle pupae, gold-ribbed hare's-ear nymphs, pheasant-tail nymphs, prince nymphs, and caddis-larvae imitations should be at hand. In addition, traditional wet flies can be very effective in this stream. The hare's-ear wet, starling and peacock, and partridge and yellow are favourites of many anglers.

To go down after the big brown trout tucked under log-jams, large streamer patterns with a lot of movement are a good bet. Patterns that use marabou or rabbit strips can be the ticket to hooking up with fish that are surprisingly large for such a small stream. There are big resident brown trout that call Whitemans home, and migratory rainbow trout, or steelhead that use Whitemans as a spawning area. These steelhead can arrive early in the fall or stay late in the spring and frequently trout anglers get a big surprise when their tiny offering is taken by a large rainbow. To target these steelhead, anglers should fish during the first few days of the trout season in late April to find steelhead that have not yet started back to the lake or get on the water a day or two after a good thunderstorm in late August or September. It is fun to hook up with such big fish in a small river, but don't expect to land many of them. With the number of obstructions found in Whitemans Creek, the odds are certainly in favour of a good-sized fish.

Due to the size of the stream, and the overgrown banks and frequent log-jams, a shorter fly rod is usually best for placing flies accurately and avoiding constant back-cast snags. A 2 m (7 ft) #4 rod is perfect for this stream, but if you don't have a rod this short, don't worry, just be ready to donate a few more flies to the bushes. The heavier #4 line for this size of creek is a compromise that will allow you to turn some of the bigger fish you may encounter.

Through the summer, anglers often find a huge abundance of small

Juvenile rainbow trout in Whitemans Creek.

rainbow trout. These are what many call "steelhead in training." Be careful with these smolts, as they are a major contributor to the steelhead fishery in the Grand River and Lake Erie. When you catch them, treat them carefully as you release them. These fish are usually from 13 to 20 cm (5 to 8 in), and their sheer abundance makes them a good choice for building confidence in beginning fly anglers. Handle and release them with care since you never know which of these smolts will return as a 2-to-5 kg (5-to-8 lb) fish in a couple of years.

Anglers using spinning gear should use small spinners, jigs, and minnow baits to work deeper pools and under log-jams. Make sure the rod and line used has the ability to turn a good fish that wants to head back for cover. Small spinners are also effective with rainbow trout of varying sizes. For bait, check that the area you are fishing is not covered by special regulations. There are areas where bait is not allowed. Worms and egg sacs fished under a float or simply with a split shot pinched a few inches above are the most popular baits.

WHITEMANS CREEK HATCH CHART

Insect	Apr 1-30	May 1-15	May 16-31	June 1-15	June 16-30	July 1-15	July 16-31	Aug 1-15	Aug 16-31	Sept 1-15	Sept 16-30
BWO	*	*		*	*						
Hendrickson		*	*								
Blue Quill				*	*						
Sulphur				*	*						
March Brown			*	*	*						
Yellow Drake					*						
Cahill				*	*	*	*	*	*	*	
Trico						*	*	*			
White Dun								*	*	*	
Tan Caddis				*	*						
Green Caddis		*	*								
Black Caddis						*	*	*	*		
Yellow Stone				*							
Brown Stone				*	*	*					

This chart identifies when these insects are active and when anglers may wish to use artificial flies to imitate them.

WATER LEVELS: Average low summer flows in Whitemans Creek are 1.7 cms (60 cfs). For current river conditions call the River Information Line at

519-621-2763 or www.grandriver.ca.

SIGHTS TO SEE: Apps' Mill Nature Centre is a GRCA outdoor education facility with classes attending daily from local schools. It is also available for bookings by community groups and offers seasonal family programs. The historic mill that provides its name is still standing, although closed to visitors. Hiking trails wind through the attractive Carolinian forest.

Nearby attractions include Brant Conservation Area, with camping and swimming facilities, the City of Brantford, and the Town of Paris.

FOR MORE INFORMATION: Apps' Mill Nature Centre 519-752-0655
GRCA at 519-621-2763 or online at www.grandriver.ca

WHAT YOU CAN DO TO MAKE THE GRAND FISHERY BETTER

Take a kid fishing.

Join a local conservation club and get involved with local projects.

Respect natural vegetation buffers and plant native trees, shrubs, and grasses on your property or along watercourses.

Please "limit your harvest" versus "harvest your limit" when fishing the Grand.

Don't mow vegetation right up to the edge of small streams or the river.

Limit use of fertilizers and pesticides on your property.

Practice water conservation in your house and business.

Never empty bait buckets into the river.

Mulch your grass when cutting and don't dump yard waste on vacant land or riverbanks.

Prevent leakage of gas and oil from cars, tractors, lawnmowers, and other machinery.

Limit lawn watering, and only water early and late in the day during dry periods.

Reduce the amount of salt used on driveways and sidewalks in winter.

Index